HISTORY OF MUSIC IN SAN FRANCISCO SERIES
VOLUME ONE: JANUARY, 1939

MUSIC
of the
GOLD RUSH
ERA

282487

AMS PRESS
NEW YORK

TYPES OF MUSIC SUNG IN
EARLY SAN FRANCISCO AND VICINITY

INDIAN SONG

Hay daily daily da, Hay daily daily da, Hay day yola mato.
Pomo Love Song

GREGORIAN CHANT

Sanc - - tus; Sanctus: Sanc - - tus, Do - - mi - nus
Sanctus, Adaptation

SPANISH SERENADE

La no-che 'sta se - re - na, Tran-qui-lo el a-qui-lon
La Noche 'Sta Serena

FORTY-NINERS' BALLAD

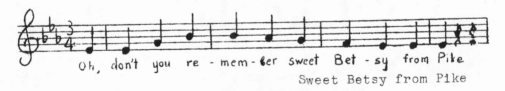

Oh, don't you re - mem-ber sweet Bet-sy from Pike
Sweet Betsy from Pike

OPERATIC ARIA

Ah! non cre-dea mi-rar - - ti Si pre-sto e-stin-to, o fio - - re;
La Sonnambula, Act III, Sc.2

WORKS PROGRESS ADMINISTRATION
Northern California
San Francisco

VOLUME ONE

MUSIC OF THE GOLD RUSH ERA

Cornel Lengyel, Editor
January, 1939
San Francisco

W.P.A. 10377   HISTORY OF MUSIC PROJECT   O.P. 665-08-3-80
Prepared with assistance of the Works Progress Administration
of California; sponsored by the City and County San Francisco.

Library of Congress Cataloging in Publication Data

History of Music Project.
    Music of the gold rush era.

    (History of music in San Francisco series, v. 1)
    Reprint of the 1939 ed.
    Bibliography: leaf
    1. Music--California--San Francisco. I. Title.
II. Title: Gold rush era, Music of the. III. Series.
ML200.8.S2H4 vol. 1, 1972   780'.9794'61 s 74-38305
ISBN 0-404-07241-0

Reprinted from the edition of 1939, San Francisco
First AMS edition published in 1972
Manufactured in the United States of America

International Standard Book Number:
Complete Set: 0-404-07240-2
Volume I   : 0-404-07241-0

Library of Congress Catalog Card Number:74-38305

AMS PRESS INC.
NEW YORK,N.Y. 10003

WORKS PROGRESS ADMINISTRATION
HISTORY OF MUSIC PROJECT
San Francisco

MUSIC OF THE GOLD RUSH ERA

Table of Contents

Few cities in America have had such intensely vari-
egated musical life as early San Francisco. Few have fostered and maintained its vital civic interest in the art.
Nearly a century ago San Francisco became a mecca for musicians; today, the City subsidizes a municipal opera, opera
house, chorus, band, and symphony. In richness of background,
New York and New Orleans can alone be compared with it. New
England took over one hundred and fifty years to arrive at
the stage which the new frontier town in El Dorado reached
within its first decade.

During the delirious days of 1849, San Francisco
became a miniature melting pot in the West. With avid interest the world's eyes were focused on the golden town which was
being stormed by soldiers of fortune from every portion of
the globe. But gold, though most important, was not the
only cause for its bursting into music. The revolutionary
mood which seized Europe in 1848 had its reverberations in
America's music halls: its aftermath, the reactionary purge
in Germany which drove Wagner and Heine into exile, sent a
large number of emigrants, including many fine musicians, to
the New World, where they founded important musical organizations. Most of the early music societies in San Francisco
were established by Germans.

An amazing period, the Gold Rush era, with all its
turbulence, crime, passion, and exaggeration, laid the foundation for the City's cultural life and serves as a fitting

index to its musical directory.

Celebrities came from almost the very beginning --
with or without Barnum's blessing. And the prima donnas,
pianists, harpists, and players of the violin were more often
than not hailed with golden showers. Curious customs pre-
vailed. Firemen were apparently the City's foremost patrons
of music. They frequently gave balls, sponsored benefits,
and paid as high as $1150.00 for a concert ticket. When Kate
Hayes arrived, they unhitched the horses from her carriage and
drew her triumphantly through the streets to her hotel. Most
of the numerous churches had their own choirs; choral societies were exceedingly popular. The Turner Gesang Verein,for
instance, in 1854 boasted six thousand members. Bands, minstrels, makers of guitars and accordions, music teachers, and
a hundred more sons and step sons of Apollo were busy in the
City.

A heightened sense of living, an intense expectancy,
a Renaissance air of terror and triumph pervaded the atmosphere. Cut-throats and newly rich millionaires were plenti-
ful. But a Lorenzo who could stir and stimulate creative
energies was lacking. There is record of penny poets, ballad-
makers, and a few native composers, but no great original music was produced in these stirring times, no great poem, play,
picture.

Pleasure was fiercely sought. If music be the
devil's invention, then Barbary Coast with its hundreds of

riotous melodeons was a most fitting place for Lucifer's rehearsals. More music was performed and more murder commit-
ted in San Francisco during this decade than in any other
city in America. One might speculate on the relation of
crime to culture.

To the genteel concert-goer of the fifties the music of the day was perhaps too harshly diversified, too dis-
connected, and made a medley too cacophonous for complete
appreciation. But distance helps the composition. It is the
purpose of this volume, Music of the Gold Rush Era, to un-
ravel a few of the decade's leading themes and to present
from a hundred years' perspective the pattern which appears.

C. L.

FOURTH OF JULY FESTIVAL, 1851, PORTSMOUTH PLAZA
(Note music store upper left.)

VIEW OF THE PLAZA OF SAN-FRANCISCO,
On the 4th of July 1851.

CHAPTER ONE: <u>MUSIC AT MISSION DOLORES</u>

ission Dolores, and indeed San Francisco
itself, owes its existence   to   the   dis-
covery of San Francisco Bay in November,
1769, by Portola's soldiery, followed by
the successful attempt of   Captain   Juan
Bautista de Anza to open up communication
by land from Mexican Sonora to the sea.   Leading   the   first
band of colonists to San Francisco, Anza selected a lagoon on
the shore of San Francisco Bay as the mission site, with the
Presidio and fort not far away.

Coming upon the lagoon on Friday, the feast day of
Our Lady of Sorrows, he named it Nuestra Senora de los Dolores, and to the Mother of Sorrows the Mission has been ac-
credited ever since, although its official title is the Mission of San Francisco de Asis.

The first mass was sung on the site of the Mission,
to the intense curiosity of the natives who came with gifts
of mussels and wild seed for the newcomers.   Moraga, left by
Anza to complete the settlement, together with the Mission
Fathers, received the Indians with presents of beads and
food.

In quick order after the arrival of the San Carlos from Monterey with artisans and supplies, camp was built for the commander, a warehouse for supplies, a chapel for mass and a group of houses for the soldiers.

The Presidio was formally taken over on September 17, 1776, appropriately on the Feast of the Impression of the Stigmata of Our Seraphic Father Saint Francis, the patron of the port.

In the following month, the completion of the mission was celebrated. Father Palou, writing an account of the consecration and dedication, deplores the lack of an organ and other musical instruments, but reflects with small satisfaction that noise-making devices took the place of music:

> "There was a continual discharge of fire-arms
> during the ceremony; and the want of incense,
> of which there was none, was supplied by the
> smoke of the muskets." 1

INDIAN CHOIR-SINGERS

Before long the Indians had rendered themselves indispensable, assuming all the manual labor essential to the orderly development of this frontier community.

They quickly matriculated as farmers, herdsmen, carpenters, blacksmiths, masons, weavers, millwrights, tanners, shoemakers, saddlers, potters and ribbonmakers. Mission

---

1 Palou, Fray Francisco, O. F. M. Historical Memoirs of New California (Berkeley: Ed. by Herbert Eugene Bolton, U.C.Press, 1926).

Dolores was particularly noted for its fine specimens of pottery.

Almost overnight the mission buildings, like mushrooms, grew and multiplied; the churches, refectories, workshops and granaries being built of materials often transported for many miles on the shoulders of the untiring Indians.

The transformation from savage to ardent neophyte, disciplined into a daily, fixed routine, imbued with newly acquired pastoral and industrial skill, "taught to read and write, instructed in music, accustomed to the service of the church, partaking of its sacraments and indoctrinated in the Christian religion," [1] testifies eloquently to the patience and capacity of mentor and pupil alike.

Into this strange new world unfolding to the native Indian, a world into which he had at first entered so timorously, and later espoused with an almost pathetic eagerness, he brought a contribution of his own -- a lithe, rhythmic grace of movement, and a weird, musical rhythm, not the music of the Gregorian chant, nor yet of the secular world, but one that nevertheless stirred the pulse, fired the imagination.

The change of seasons, the worship of the Great Spirit, the fact of birth and death, the matter of war and victory -- all found appropriate expression in the music of the early California Indians.

---

1 Dwinell, John Whipple. The Colonial History of San Francisco (San Francisco: Towne and Bacon, 1863).

Drums, rattles, bone whistles, sufficed to produce the haunting music accompanying the ritual of the Indian tribes. Dr. Derrick N. Lehmer of Berkeley, who has recorded some of these chants, discerns what he calls a "lilting, lyric" quality in the musical notes, a wild pathos in their death chants, and a general underlying poetic feeling hitherto unsuspected. The Bancroft Library at the University of California has a manuscript collection of this music.

Because of the ineradicable instinct of the native Indian for some form of musical expression, and the deft, imitative faculty of the untutored -- under the skilled guidance of the Mission Fathers, the transition from "heathen" ritualistic chant to the Gregorian chant and the singing of the Mass was accomplished with comparative ease.

There was much competition among the musical aspirants of the tribes, the Indians regarding it an honor to be allowed to participate in the ceremonials of the church.

THE GREGORIAN CHANT

Practically all of the missions had their well-trained choirs. Whether raised in unison, intoning the solemn Gregorian chant or some majestic choral of the Church, or singing popular ballads on feast days, the sonorous if somewhat guttural voices of the neophytes, equally at home in the Spanish and Latin tongue, evoked the enthusiastic praise of all who visited the missions.

Robert Louis Stevenson, attending the annual festival of San Carlos, held in the ruined Mission of Carmelo, writes of the choral singing of a number of the Indians who were still lingering in the neighborhood they had known as home:

> "....the Indians troop together, their bright dresses contrasting with their dark and melancholy faces....An Indian, stone blind and about eighty years of age, conducts the singing; other Indians compose the choir; yet they have the Gregorian music at their finger ends, and pronounce the Latin so correctly that I could follow the music as they sang....I have never seen faces more vividly lit up with joy than the faces of these Indian singers. It was to them not only the worship of God, nor an act by which they recalled and commemorated better days, but was besides an exercise of culture, where all they knew of art and letters was united and expressed...." 1

These facile converts had not only a remarkable ear for music, but displayed equal talent in reading the notes which, anachronistic to the modern eye, were written in the form of squares or diamonds, on a stave of four or five, sometimes six lines, in distinguishing colors of yellow, red, white and black, to guide the choristers through the intricacies of their respective parts.

It is to the painstaking and delicate work of Fray Estaban Tapis, President of the missionaries from 1803 to 1812, that the missions owed many of their quaintly written scores of the "Alabado " (Song of Praise), the antiphonal, and other musical offices of the Church. Some of these scripts are still extant in varying states of preservation.

---

1 Stevenson, Robert Louis. Across the Plains with Other Memories and Essays (London: Chatto and Windus, 1910).

In a little room at the Mission of San Luis Rey, amid a few broken old relics, rests Father Peyri's "Music Book," a huge hide-bound volume, some two feet square. It is an excellent specimen of mission work, with great square notes in black and red, its huge lettering inscribed on yellow, crumbling vellum.

Only recently at San Juan Capistrano two complete scores of the music of a mass entitled "La Misa Catalana" have been discovered intact in the possession of a parishioner. This mass, composed by the celebrated Fray Narciso Duran of the Mission of San Jose, was frequently sung at all of the various missions.

The authors of The California Padres and Their Missions speak of the wonderful memory of the Indians, to a handful of whom is owed the preservation of some of the hymns, chants and chorals that were most regularly sung at the mission services.

One veteran Indian, Fernando Cardenas, familiarly known as Fernandito (little Fernando), sang a number of the well-remembered chants to Father Alexander Buckler, priest of Mission Santa Ines, who has preserved them in phonographic records. They include the "Alabado" --

> "A hymn ever on the lips of priest and neophyte, not alone at the services in the missions, but on trips of exploration, sung when breaking camp before the day's march, or even used as a salutation in ordinary greeting."

Delighted with the vocal prowess of their pupils, the Padres further initiated them in the intricacies of instrumental music.

The chief difficulty lay in obtaining the proper instruments, owing to the inaccessibility of the cultural centers in Mexico and Spain. However, the resourceful natives solved this problem (as they had overcome so many other obstacles) by manufacturing most of their musical instruments.

PRIMITIVE ORCHESTRAS

The single violin accompanying practice and rehearsals at Mission Dolores was soon elevated to the dignity of "first violin" in an orchestra of four pieces.

Otto von Kotzebue, sailor-scientist, commander of the Russian ship Rurik, visiting the mission in 1816, comments on the Church orchestra comprising "a violin, violoncello and two flutes," which Father Engelhardt reports had by 1827 increased by "8 violins, 2 violones and 2 drums." [1]

San Gabriel Mission presaged the use of the brasses, flutes, guitars and violins in addition to drums, triangles and cymbals. San Jose likewise employed home-made drums, adding trumpets as well to the violins and flutes of its thirty-piece orchestra.

Fray Narciso Duran, Padre of San Jose, and composer as well as director of music, was a picturesque figure.

---

[1] Engelhardt, O.F.M. Fr. Zephyrin. San Francisco or Mission Dolores (Chicago: Franciscan Herald Press, 1924).

He is pictured as beating time against one of the pillars of the corridor with one hand, and wiping the perspiration from his brow with the other as he conducted rehearsals of his motley orchestra in the large square of the mission, calling an instant halt of the performance on detection of the slightest discordant note.

San Luis Rey, not to be outdone, under one of the ablest and most energetic of all the Franciscans Padre Antonio Peyri, numbered forty pieces in its Indian "band."

But to Santa Clara goes the distinction of housing the most spectacular of all the mission orchestras. These musicians had grown far beyond the stage of playing by note, displaying exceptional skill not only in execution but in the arrangement of their notes.

De Mofras, celebrated French explorer, on the occasion of a visit to Santa Clara, tells of their "resplendent French uniforms," doubtless acquired from one of the trading ships. He records his astonishment on attending mass to hear the orchestra break out with the martial strains of "La Marseillaise," at the moment of the elevation of the Host, and later accompany the procession with the old French air, "Vive Henri Quatre."

The Padre told his visitor of the pride of the musicians in the little organ that had been imported for the mission from France, and how, whether inoculated or not with its Gallic spirit, they were apt at any time, with more zeal

than discretion to break out in martial airs, waltzes or
lively polkas, regardless of the solemnity of the occasion.

In the cool of early evening, their daily tasks accomplished and rigid discipline relaxed, the Indian band assembled under the canopy of the stars in the open squares of
the missions, precursors, perhaps, of the modern open-air
"shell" or "bowl," and gave concerts of their own selection
for the delectation of their brethern. Such were the modest
progenitors of California's orchestral music.

CHAPTER TWO: <u>FANDANGOS AND FIESTAS</u>

 ife on the ranchos of California reached the height of spontaneous gaiety, gracious hospitality and romantic charm in the period 1828 to 1846 under the flag of the Mexican Republic. The asceticism of the missions gave way to the pleasure-loving, easy-going rancheros, "whiling away the late hours of the day and the early hours of the night, in an almost continuous fiesta of romance."

Spain, the mother country, jealous of her prerogatives had doled out her few land grants with a niggardly hand. But Mexico, her estranged offspring, particularly in the latter part of the period when it became evident that California would pass to the control of the United States, gradually adopted a more liberal policy, and the hundred or more ranchos prodigally deeded by the Mexican government spread their rolling areas from the Pacific to the San Joaquin.

The establishments of the wealthier rancheros took on the aspect of the European feudal estates of the middle ages, each with its overlord, his major-domo or steward, and frequently, whole tribes of Indian retainers.

The present site of Oakland, Alameda and Berkeley constituted only a portion of what was once the Rancho San Antonio, the property of Don Luis Peralta, while General Mariano Guadalupe Vallejo, once the richest man in the province, possessed great tracts of land in Sonoma County, maintaining a small army of Indians in the field, in addition to fifty or more house servants.

Intermarriage occurred to such an extent among the small population of the province that before long practically everybody was related to everybody else.

Family life, replete with dignity and ceremony, was characterized by a rare warmth of affectionate devotion; there was never a happier family than when the ranchero saw his sons and sons' sons bringing their wives to the paternal roof, adding to the seats of the ever lengthening table.

Dr. Platon Vallejo writes:

"Hospitality was the freest thing in the world in the old pastoral days. There were no week-end limitations. Your guests arrived and at once your house and appurtenances became theirs.

"In the daytime the men mounted their horses, inspecting the herds and work of the fields. The women stayed at home, sewed, gossiped, ate more or less 'dulces' or sweets, and had a quiet, congenial good time.

"The evenings were given over to pure merriment. Every hacienda had its stringed band of several pieces, the harp, which the women played exceptionally well, the guitar, violin and occasionally a clarinet or flute. Every night rain or shine, except in times of death or sorrow, there was a baile." 1

1 Vallejo, Guadalupe. Notes on California Rancho and Mission Life Century Magazine. Vol. XIX.

THE FIRST PIANO LESSON

There were only three pianos in the province, brought from Baltimore by Captain Smith and sold, one each to Jose Abrego, Eulogio Celis in San Pedro, and the third to General Vallejo in Sonoma, but since none had the slightest notion how to play upon the instrument, their acquisition remained a matter of pride if not of aesthetic use, until the accidental coming to the rancho of General Vallejo of an itinerant German musician, Andrew Hoeppner, in the year 1846.

This proved a fortuitous circumstance for both host and guest, for to the delight of the Vallejo household the German played the pianoforte so effectively that he was urged to remain as tutor to the General, his wife and all of their sixteen children. An agreement was concluded whereby the tutor after five years' residence, or longer if necessary, was to receive in exchange for his musical tuition, a very considerable grant of land and money.

In the forthright, naive code of the Spanish Californians, pleasure to a considerable extent, held equal rank with the harsher utilities of life, "for without enjoyment a race would speedily degenerate."

With the aptitude for music inherent in the Latin race, song came as readily to their lips as the air they breathed. He who could neither sing nor play upon some musical instrument was considered only half a man. They had particularly pleasing baritone or tenor voices and did not as a rule sing in the strange, high falsetto affected in Mexico.

CANTICLES AND BALLAD-MAKERS

The ballads sung were not transcribed and set to music but, in the manner of folk songs, spread by word of mouth. Some of this music has been rescued from oblivion and published in printed form.

The Californians used the musical idiom of their Spanish and Mexican forbears supplemented by melodic composition and improvisation of their own, ranging from verses of ardent fervor to barbed shafts of satire and ridicule aimed against the political and social foibles of their time.

Their tireless activities frequently began with the break of day, when the entire household, including the Indian servants, joined in singing this reverential salute to the day.

El Cantico Del Alba

Ya viene el alba,
Rayando el dia;
Digamos todos
Ave Maria.

Now comes the dawn,
Brightening to the day.
Hail, Mary, hail,
Let us all say.

Nacio Maria
Para consuelo
De pecadores,
Y luz del cielo.

Born was Mary
For Heaven's light
And help of sinners
In their plight.

Digamos todos
Con eficacia
Nacio Maria
Llena de gracia.

Let us all sing;
Help of our race
Was Mary born,
And full of grace.

Fue sola hermosa,
Sola Maria,
La Que acompana
La luz del dia.

Alone in beauty,
Unequaled one,
Mary, thou comest
Fair as the sun. 1

---

1 Saunders, Charles Francis. The California Padres and Their Missions (New York: Houghton-Mifflin Co., 1915).

The study of the folk songs of a people, while more imaginative than factual, serves none the less to recreate the atmosphere and social conditions under which they lived. This is particularly true of the mercurial Latin races whose volatile emotions found constant and ready utterance in song.

The ballads of the Spanish Californians combined gaiety and pathos with an elaborate ornamentation and extravagance of phrase frequently showing traces of the Arab and Moorish influence persisting in old Spain.

A peaceable, indolent, pleasure-loving race, they did not praise war; nor oddly enough, although a nation of wine drinkers, had they any typical wine songs, Simple in melody, rich in feeling, Charles Fletcher Lummis finds these songs "in word, air, grace, fire, wit and rhythm, superior to many art-songs and to the commercial shoddy produced at a later era."

Throughout the day and the greater part of the night that followed, music symbolized every conscious act of the ranchero and his family. The events of birth, love, courtship and marriage, making up the placid cycle of their days, all had their appropriate musical ceremonial.

The baptism of an infant, whether the first or the twentieth in the family, was the occasion for joyous festivity. The procession from the home of the padrinos or godparents to that of the parents, and thence to the parish church, assumed the proportions of a cavalcade, to the accompaniment of music, the firing of rockets and ringing of bells, which, continuing all the way back, preluded celebration with music lasting one or two days.

THE TROUBADOUR'S GUITAR

The serenade was an indispensable feature of the ceremony of courtship in the customs of the rancheros. General Vallejo relates that "it was considered very improper for a girl to receive a proposal of marriage before her parents had been consulted by the lover or his parents."

As the youthful pair chafed at the seemingly endless deliberations of their elders, the impatient suitor had no other recourse than to pour out his heart beneath the latticed window of the girl whose favor he sought.

The custom of the serenade continued long after American occupation. It was still in vogue as late as 1880, when Robert Louis Stevenson wrote of a visit to Monterey:

> "Night after night serenaders would be going
> about the street, sometimes in company, com-
> bining voices and instruments, sometimes sev-
> erally, each guitar before a different window.
> It was a strange thing to lie awake in nine-
> teenth century America and hear the guitar ac-
> company, and one of these old, heart-breaking
> Spanish love songs mount into the night air." 1

The parents' consent finally obtained, and the necessary formalities concluded, the bridal party marched silently to church, without music; but after the ceremony,

---

1 Stevenson, Robert Louis. Across the Plains with Other Memories and Essays (London: Chatto and Windus, 1910).

friends received them at the door with music, and bore them home in triumph. If the pair lived at a distance in the country, another band of musicians met them half-way, and all proceeded to the rancho where an arbor protecting the hard earth floor from the weather had been prepared for the dance, which lasted sometimes a week or more, the guests taking turns at relieving the musicians who remained throughout the celebration.

The Indian orchestras from the missions were in constant demand to play at weddings and all other functions of the rancheros. The same Indians who had assisted in the mass of the morning, and perhaps added the notes of their violins, flutes and drums to the din of a bull and bear fight in the afternoon, would be called upon to furnish the music for the dance at night. And they did it well, being much more accustomed, even with their church music, to lively and inspiriting operatic airs and dancing tunes, than to slow and lugubrious elegies and dirges.

The program usually consisted of 'contradanzas, min-uets, Aragonese jotas, and various other dances usual among the Spanish population. It was the custom to accompany the dancing with the singing of appropriate verses frequently im-provised on the spur of the moment." 1

---

1 Historia de California   Mss. Bancroft Collection,   U. C., Berkeley, Calif.

The music at the wedding of Vallejo, later command-
ante of the Port of San Francisco, attended by the Governor
and his suite and by all the ranchero celebrities from far
and wide, was mainly furnished by one of these Indian orchestras.

WASHDAY FIESTA

Even the modest wash-day was the occasion of a
fiesta lasting sometimes as long as a week. It was a commun-
al affair with whole families and their servants repairing to
the nearest natural springs or waterholes into which the
clothes, saturated with home-made soap, were dipped then
rubbed on smooth rocks until they were a glistening white,
and spread out to dry on the tops of low bushes. As usual,
music, dancing, and feasting played a major part in the
prolonged outing. The Americans called one of these springs
"The Washerwomen's Canon."

THE JOTA, ZORRITA AND FANDANGO

In earlier days the dancers disbanded at ten or
eleven o'clock at night, but soon such early hours began to
be disregarded and the merrymaking continued through consecutive days and nights with sporadic sleep snatched at intervals. They thought nothing of riding all day to attend a
baile at some distant rancho. Duflot de Mofras, the Frenchman who visited the coast in 1841, accompanied a party of
thirty from Sonoma to a rancho many miles removed. They

started in the morning, arrived in the evening, danced all that night, the next day and the following night, and on the third day started at sunrise on their homeward journey.

In the early days folk dances with set figures were the rule but later the waltz, polka, mazurka and other European "round dances" were introduced. The waltz was interdicted by the clergy but reintroduced in 1830 with the sanction of the governor of the province.

The jota was the favorite among the folk dances. It resembled the American Virginia reel and was accompanied by the singing of verses, with a refrain at which the hands of the dancers were linked chain-fashion.

Other dances of intricate steps, accompanied by singing and recital of verses generally improvised with much readiness and wit, were "el zorrita (little fox), el camotes (sweet potatoes), el borrego (the lamb), el caballo (the horse), and el burro (the donkey). The burro was almost the counterpart of the American 'Old Dan Tucker.'" 1

One of the most popular dances was called el canastita de flores (the little basket of flowers) in which the dancers formed a ring, singing as they circled. The last word of the song was the signal for the men to rush forward and embrace the partner selected. If the number chanced to be uneven, the disconsolate "wallflower," standing alone, became the "duena de las burlas" (the dame of the joke.)

_____

1 Sanchez, Nellie Van de Grift. Spanish Arcadia (San Francisco: Powell Publishing Co., 1929.)

In the fandango which was danced by a man and woman, to the accompaniment of castanets, the music would suddenly stop and the singer would cry out "bomba!" At this signal one or the other of the partners was required to improvise the next verse which was usually marked by great variety and originality.

Carnival week, preceding Lent, was marked by the cascarone balls -- a feature of social life as characteristic of the California of that day as the Mardi Gras of Europe.

With the gaiety underlying even their serious moments, the most solemn religious festivals were stripped of the least semblance of puritanical gloom.

> "Christmas, the great festival of the year, and La Noche Buena (the good night) were celebrated with much pomp. After the midnight mass a sacred drama, called Los Pastores (The Shepherds), representing the Bible story, was performed by a party of young persons dressed in appropriate costumes. The whole performance was enlivened by the notes of the guitar, and interspersed with songs and comic incidents that seemed better adapted to the stage than the church." [1]

Of these generous, confiding, music-loving people it was said that after the American conquest more was accomplished in winning their confidence and friendship by the military bands of the United States forces than by proclamations. The bands played in the open plazas each night at sunset, drawing first the children and then their elders. Even the rancheros from considerable distances came and stayed to listen.

---

[1] Sanchez, Nellie Van de Grift. Spanish Arcadia (San Francisco: Powell Publishing Co., 1929.)

The old priest sitting by the church door remarked that "music will do more service in the conquest of California than a thousand bayonets."

The idyllic life on the ranchos was soon to come to an end, however, after the discovery of gold. With the coming of the hordes of miners and adventurers, life increased its tempo from andante to gallop. Now was a new day, bringing new people, new customs, a furious new energy. The languid guitar of the troubadour was displaced by the strident twang of the miner's banjo. The canticle to the rising sun was displaced by the lusty verses of "Oh, Susanna." San Francisco was one day a pastoral Spanish Rancho, and the next it was the Barbary Coast.

CHAPTER THREE: BARBARY COAST MELODEONS

he Yankee, James W. Marshall, by his discovery of gold at Coloma on the grant of
Captain John Sutter in January, 1848 made
world history. It required neither radio,
telephone nor air-mail to speed the thrill-
ing news to the four corners of the earth.
When word of the epochal discovery of the yellow
metal was confirmed in the erstwhile Yerba Buena, only the
year before officially named San Francisco, Eldredge   describes the excitement as "prodigious," and in a few days
the exodus had begun. By boat, by mule and horse, or on foot
they went, all eager to reach the mines, fearful that the
gold would be gone before they could get there to receive
their share.

> "Business houses closed their doors. There was
> no service in the little church on the plaza,
> and a padlock was on the door of the alcalde's
> office. The ships in the harbor were deserted
> alike by masters and sailors. Soldiers deserted
> their posts and fled, taking arms, horses,
> blankets with them; others were sent after them
> to force them back to duty, and all, pursuers
> and pursued, went to the mines together." 1

---

1 Eldredge, Zoeth Skinner. The Beginnings of San Francisco
(Zoeth S. Eldredge, San Francisco, 1912.)

By May 1, 1848 at least two thousand men were "scratching like hens in the sand and gravel of the Sacramento Valley," tripled and quadrupled in numbers by the arrival of Mexicans and the natives of other Central and South American countries. Swarming competitors traveling overland by way of the Sierras on foot, on horseback or by wagon train, were out-raced by the passengers on the Steamship California, first of the Pacific Mail steamers to anchor off Yerba Buena Cove with her cargo of gold-hunters from the Eastern and Southern states. This was in February, 1849. In less than a year after the arrival of this first contingent of immigrants, between forty and fifty thousand men had passed through the Golden Gate on their way to the gold fields.

At least five hundred ships, denuded of their crews, became stranded in the harbor. Many of them never sailed again, but rotted away and sank at their moorings. Still others were drawn up on the beach and turned into saloons and boarding houses, remaining in long use after the filling in of the cove had begun.

"One, the clipper ship Niantic, was sunk in shallow water about where Clay and Sansome Streets now intersect, and became the foundation of the Niantic Hotel, a favorite hostelry of the early days." 1

Between the years of 1836 and 1850, the population of San Francisco had increased from less than fifty families

---

1 Eldredge, Zoeth Skinner. The Beginnings of San Francisco (Zoeth S. Eldredge, San Francisco, 1912.)

to twenty-five thousand persons, most of whom were adult males under fifty. They were men of every nationality, of every hue and type of raiment, each speaking the tongue of his native land, all adding to the tumult and babel of confusion.

WHY THEY DID NOT STAY AT HOME

Leady canvas tents or hastily constructed board shanties with muslin partitions served to house the majority of these newcomers. The lodging houses and even the more pretentious hotels consisted for the most part of one or more large rooms with rows of bunks fastened to the walls and lines of hard cots on the floor at fifteen dollars a night. The few private rooms available rented for three hundred to one thousand dollars a month, payable in advance. Sleeping space on tables, benches, chairs, bare floors went at a premium -- all infested with vermin and the huge rodents that overran the town, a heritage from the rotting ships in the harbor. Gaping holes in the makeshift highways made passage a menace, and men, horses, mules and carts were sucked down into the mud with considerable loss of life.

> "Here was no community growing slowly and patiently into coherence. It was a thing of instantaneous birth with every beauty and every ugliness that normally takes time to achieve... the hunger for gold filled the erstwhile village of Yerba Buena with cut-throats, Methodist ministers, gamblers, South-sea whalers, university professors, frontier men, French marquises, Chinese coolies, Chilean landowners, Australian convicts and Philadelphia Quakers.

> "In an eye's twinkling the new city by the Gold-
> en Gate became squalid, pretentious, immoral,
> high-minded, extravagant, prudent, evil, heroic
> --all in one breath." 1

All of this motley crowd nightly thronged the gaming tables -- they sought relaxation and escape from the in-
tolerable conditions surrounding their fetid, overcrowded
lodgings. In the grip of the wild, speculative fever that
drove them to the "diggings," they craved amusement, excitement, life keyed to its highest pitch.

The mild interest evinced in the circus, first public entertainment in San Francisco after the beginning of the
gold rush, soon subsided. Gambling became and remained the
principal diversion of the great mass of restless, turbulent,
gold-hungry men who almost over night had transformed, in Dobie's words, "the once peaceful hamlet of San Francisco into a
bawdy, bustling bedlam of mud-holes and shanties." 1

"DENS OF INIQUITY"

Portsmouth Square, the old Plaza of Mexican days,
was the gambling center of the town. With the exception of a
few hotels and small stores, it was given over entirely to
buildings devoted exclusively to gambling, while tables were
also available for play in the saloons and in the barrooms of
hotels. All operated day and night, seven days a week, as
did many other establishments in the side streets and along

---

1 Dobie, Charles Caldwell. San Francisco: A Pageant (New
York, London: D. E. Appleton-Century Co., 1933.)

the waterfront, and from all came sounds of music in "full blast, as though pandemonium were let loose."

The "dens of iniquity" against which the Reverend William Taylor, celebrated street preacher, unloosed the vials of his evangelistic wrath, included the far famed Bella Union, the El Dorado, the Parker House, Dennison's Exchange, the Empire, the Mazourka, the Arcade, the Varsouvienne, the Ward House, La Sociedad, the Fontine House, the St. Charles, the Alhambra, the Verandah and the Aguila de Oro, all on or closely bordering Portsmouth Square. Bill Briggs' place in Montgomery Street near Pine, and Steve Whipple's house in Commercial Street, later occupied by the Pacific Club, were among the better known just off the Square, with hundreds of second-rate establishments found in the less frequented streets. In those early days the number of gambling houses was estimated at approximately a thousand, all giving out the sound of music varying in quality with the social status of its source. (For Melodeons, See Appendix A.)

In the noisy dance halls along Pacific Street, the guitars, tambourines, and fiddles never rested. Here, in promiscuous melee, were men and women of all nations, complexions, and professions.

> "Lascar, Brazilian, Chilean, Mulatto, Nantucket whalemen, Englishmen and native Californians. Light-haired Yankee touched glasses with swart Chilean, and both bought drinks from the slim, dark-eyed girls who danced and sang to the constant heel-tapping which accompanied the music." [1]

---

[1] Asbury, Herbert. Barbary Coast (New York: Alfred A. Knopf, 1933.)

THE EL DORADO

The El Dorado, adjoining the Parker House at Washington and Kearny Streets, where the Hall of Justice now stands, was originally a canvas tent, fifteen by twenty-five feet. This was soon replaced by a large square room of rough boards with convenient alcoves partitioned off by muslin curtains to permit momentary dalliance between intervals of the game.

The gambling room was elegantly furnished and decorated, ablaze with light from a dozen crystal chandeliers. At one end was a raised platform draped, with bunting and flags, on which an orchestra played without cessation, music ranging from Mendelssohn and Strauss to the latest dance trot.

At the other end stretched the bar, flanked with long French mirrors and richly appointed with fine crystal and silver. Refreshments, including wine and cigars, were served gratis to the players at all times.

All of this color and glitter served as an impressive front for the gaming tables lining the room, which were covered with huge piles of gold dust, nuggets, and gold and silver coins.

Hubert Howe Bancroft says of the croupier who presided over the tables, "that he is as ready with the pistol as with his toothpick, but he never uses it unless he is right; then, he will kill a man as mercilessly as he would brush a fly from his immaculate linen...."

The competitive rivalry of the more luxurious establishments, however, was not confined solely to the allurements of the game. They vied with each other in procuring the best musicians available as soloists and members of their orchestras.

El Dorado retained its asthmatic old orchestrion along with an accomplished orchestra and gifted soloists, although the "female violinist," described by Bayard Taylor in his El Dorado, seems to have achieved fame as a gymnastic exhibitionist, rather than a musical virtuoso. He tells us of her "tasking her talent and strength of muscle, her music adding to the excitement of the play."

THE BELLA UNION

The Bella Union, on the Washington street side of the Plaza, countered with a quintet of Mexican musicians playing two harps, two guitars and a flute. "Their repertoire contained the popular waltzes and dances of the time, and many weird, curious airs of old Spain, sad refrains and amorous songs without words that suggested airs long since floating on the moonlit night in old Seville beneath the iron-latticed balconies where lovely senoritas listened with bated breath...." 1

The shining star of the Bella Union, however, was the singer and violinist Charley Schultze, the first person

1 Barry, T. A.   Men and Memories of San Francisco in the Spring of '50 (San Francisco: B. A. Patten, A. L. Bancroft and Co., 1873.)

to play in San Francisco, and probably in the United States as well, the tune of "Aloha." To this famous Hawaiian air he sang: "You Never Miss Your Sainted Mother Till She's Dead and Gone to Heaven."

The Verandah introduced a "one-man **orchestra**." Forestalling the musically ingenious trap-drummer of the modern "hot swing" band, he entertained his hilarious audiences with pipes tied to his chin, a drum strapped upon his back, drumsticks fastened to his elbows, and cymbals attached to his wrists, all played in furious tempo at the same time. To complete the cacophony he added a clumsy form of tap-dancing, patting his feet, encased in huge, hard-soled shoes, with enormous clatter upon the floor.

El Dorado's acrobatic violinist soon shared feminine honors with a French arrival at the Alhambra, whose performance, also upon the violin, netted her two ounces of gold dust or about thirty-two dollars daily.

The Aguila de Oro presented a real innovation during the autumn of 1849. Even its restless, polyglot audience was momentarily stilled by plaintive, moving spirituals introduced for the first time in San Francisco by a splendidly trained negro chorus.

BAR-ROOM BALLADS

But the loudest guffaw and the volatile tear so ready to the eye of the case-hardened gamester and hoodlum alike, were reserved for the raucous, roistering songs "that came roaring into California by land and sea, in those mad days of '49." No special invitation was needed to "give a hand" to Charles Bensel who drifted to California with the Argonauts of 1849, and under the stage name of Charles Rhodes made history with his famous song, "The Days of Old, the Days of Gold, and The Days of '49." Its melody infected the cities and mining camps, and even today is possessed of something of the aura of the State song of California:

> Here you see old Tom Moore, a relic of
>   former days;
> A bummer too, they call me now but
>   what care I for praise,
> For my heart is filled with the days of
>   old and oft do I repine
> For the days of old, and the days of gold,
>   and the days of '49.

Tapping out the rhythm with heavy, hobnailed boots, all hands joined lustily in the chorus. Another of their prime favorites, which they sang to the tune of "Pop Goes the Weasel," was

A Ripping Trip

> You go aboard a leaky boat
>   And sail for San Francisco,
> You've got to pump to keep her afloat,
>   You've got that, by jingo!
> The engine soon begins to squeak,
>   But nary a thing to oil her;
> Impossible to stop the leak,
>   Rip, goes the boiler. 1

These songs of the "grubbing landlubbers" were often out-shouted by the sailors on shore-leave, who, streaming

---

1 Lomax, John A. <u>Cowboy Songs and Other Frontier Ballads</u> (New York: The Macmillan Co., 1936.)

into the bar-rooms, dance-halls, and concert saloons,   prodigally spending their pay and not overly captious of the quality of their entertainment, were considered   specially desir-
able   "cash customers"   and for many   years provided   a large
share of the revenue flowing into the resorts of   the Barbary
Coast.

In spite of the lively competition   between the rival Houses, the Bella Union was their favorite haunt, and the
rollicking shanties that were "the very essence of their sea-
faring life,"   the rhythmic accompaniment to all   their tasks
at sea,   formed likewise   the hub   of their   entertainment on
shore.

Before   the   evening   was far   advanced some   jolly
group of "tars" were sure to stop   the show with at least one
version of "Blow, Bullies, Blow."

> A Yankee ship comes down the river,
> Blow, Boys, Blow!
> A Yankee ship and a Yankee skipper.
> Blow, my bully boys, blow! 1

The shanties of the Seven Seas   in as many tongues,
were hashed and   rehashed until the   singers, breathless from
their exertions, turned their talents in other equally stren-
uous directions.

The   Frenchman,   Albert Benard   de Russailh,   found
these dubious   gaities not   at all to   his liking.   "The San
Francisco gambling   houses are quite unlike   those of France,

---

1 Deep Sea Shanties, Old Sea Songs   Ed. by Frank Shay,   (Wm.
Heineman, Ltd., London, 1925.)

Belgium and Germany. In Europe at least, they are not low and disgusting. Fashionable people gather in luxurious halls and every one is well bred and conventional. If vice in evening-dress ever slipped in, it was not as repulsive as in San Francisco where it is clothed in rags." 1

His compatriot, Ernest de Massey, likewise comments that "it is like pandemonium let loose...as the orchestra plays its liveliest polka, and the singers air their most lurid songs accompanied by suggestive poses." 2

FIRST MINSTREL TROUPE

On October 22, 1849 came the opening performance of The Philadelphia Minstrels, the first minstrel troupe in San Francisco: "The citizens are favored by the truly amusing concerts for an admission fee of $2.00 at the Bella Union Hall, entrance on Washington Street. All lovers of fun are advised to go and hear them." 3

Among the performers was C. C. Alvered, already a renowned comedian, who shortly after became prominently identified with the San Francisco Theatre. Unfortunately,

---

1 de Russailh, Albert Benard. Last Adventure (S. F. in 1851) original journal, trans. by Clarkson Crane (The Westgate Press, 1931.)
2 de Massey, Ernest. A Frenchman in the Gold Rush (trans. by Marguerite Eyer Wilbur, Argonaut of 1849.)
3 Dobie, Charles Caldwell. San Francisco: A Pageant (New York, London: D. E. Appleton-Century Co., 1933.)

however, the performances, which were very popular and seemed destined for a long run were brought to an inauspicious end. One of the members of the troupe was killed in a brawl at the Bella Union Bar and the company hastily departed for Hawaii.

Answering the insistent demand of the more cultivated members of the community, the first "grand concert" was given at the California Exchange on Portsmouth Square on Monday afternoon, December 22, 1850.

The Alta California, on the following day, in the first real musical criticism on file in the newspapers of time, comments:

> "The first grand concert of vocal and instrumental music was given yesterday afternoon at the California Exchange. Some forty musicians performed many of the most popular and grand overtures, symphonies and variations of the composers. A number of these artists rank among the very first performers that can be named anywhere. We have heard the grand aria from 'Attila' (an opera by Handel) executed on the trombone by Signor Lobero, spoken of by excellent judges as one of the finest exhibitions of taste, science and skill ever offered to the appreciation of an audience."

The critic then descants upon the singing of the Cavatina from La Sonnambula by Senora Abalos. Slightly mixing his metaphor he describes it as "full of expression and feeling, and poured forth in a torrent of silvery sound in golden threads of attenuated melody...."

Encouraged by the enthusiastic response of critics and public to what was considered a highly experimental form of entertainment, rival establishments followed with other concerts in due course. The Louisiana Saloon gave a "French Concert" on January 30, 1851 with marked success. Great enthusiasm was manifested, the performance closing with a rousing rendition of "Yankee Doodle" and the "Marseillaise."

The growing concern of the <u>Daily Alta California</u> over the manners of the community evinced itself in an item appearing in its columns on February 3, 1851:

"Advice Gratis"

"We would respectfully advise gentlemen, if they must expectorate tobacco juice in church or at the theatre, that they should be a little particular to eject it upon their own boots and pantaloons, instead of the boots and pantaloons of others."

On June 16, 1852, the <u>Daily Alta California</u> announced:

"Madam Foubert, a great favorite with our public, will shortly commence a series of concerts at the Verandah, whose second story is being elegantly decorated, and comfort and good taste will predominate throughout.

"The concerts will be given three times a week and the choicest talent engaged. Here our citizens can enjoy some rational amusements, in which their families can partake, unaccompanied by the noise and bustle which attend places of more public resort."

PROMENADE CONCERTS

On May 9, 1852, the first of a series of "Promenade Concerts a la Julien" regarded as the forerunner of future symphony concerts, was given at the "elegant" Arcade Saloon on Commercial and Clay Streets. In the Sunday morning edition on the day of the concert, the <u>Daily Alta California</u> had announced that "some of the finest artists in the country have been engaged, and from the character of the pieces on the program, the entertainment will be one of an interesting and brilliant character."

Among the artists to appear were Madame Fulvie Bouchinett, vocal soloist, accompanied by Mr. McKorkell and Herr Schubert in his second appearance as soloist on the new instrument, the corno de bassette. Another artist, Mr. Simonson, one of the two promoters of the concert, was described by the Daily Alta California of the above date as "the young gentleman who stands without question far above any other violinist in California. He has been among us for a long time and he is well known and much admired, even by hundreds who are incapable of appreciating his powers to the fullest extent."

This effort having achieved a gratifying success, a second and more ambitious concert was forthwith advertised:

"Promenade Concerts, a la Julien--Messrs. Simonson and Peck have the pleasure to announce that their first Promenade Concert having been completely successful they will give their second Concert on Sunday evening next, May 9, at the elegant Saloon of the Arcade, Commercial and Clay Streets, on which occasion, with considerable addition to their force, they will perform a selection of the most beautiful classic and lively music; interspersed with songs, solos and a variety of new musical effect, never before heard in this country. The orchestration will consist of the following, viz: Mr. Simonson, the astonishing violinist; two pianofortes, played by those esteemed artists, Messrs. Linden and McKorkell; Mr. Ehrich, the favorite violincellist; Mr. Peck, the admirable violinist.

"The great artist, Herr Schubert, on the clarinet, and for the second time on his new and admired instrument, the corno de bassette.

"Mme. Fulvie Bouchinett, the celebrated harpist
and vocalist, is engaged and will make her second appearance at these concerts and give some
of her choicest pieces.

"N.B.--The saloon will be especially arranged
for the comfort and satisfaction of ladies and
families."

And here is the program that was presented on this

occasion:

PART I

Overture, "Cenerentola".................Rossini
Cavatina, "Robert toi que J'aime".....Meyerbeer
   Madame Fulvie Bouchinett
Solo, Violincello......................Kummer
    Mr. Ehrich

Intermission 15 minutes for promenade by the
audience.

Overture, "Guillaume Tell"..............Rossini
Mr. Schubert, whose performance on the corno
de bassetto was received with great applause
on the last concert, will play another solo.

First Concerto for the Violin.......De Beriot
Song, "Les Pocherons"..................Grisar
   Madame Fulvie Bouchinett

Intermission 15 minutes for promenade.

Overture, "Allesandro Stradella" ....Flotow
"Adelaiden Waltz"......................Strauss
Grand Duo, Harp and Pianoforte..........Labarre
  Madame Bouchinett and Mr. McKorkell
Finale........Grand Potpourri pour l'orchestra.

The Bella Union not to be outdone by her competit-

ors, advertised on February 7, 1852:

"Grand Vocal Concert with Accompaniment--to the
lovers of Music of Both Sexes--will be given
on Sunday, the 8th instant, in the fine saloon
of the Bella Union. The following pieces selected from the most brilliant operas will be
sung: Belaserio-Duetto (Donizetti); L'Elisire
d'Amore Romanza (Donizetti); English ballad--
I'm Afloat, I'm Afloat, (Russell); Sonnambula--
Cavatina (Bellini); Romeo Giuletta--Cavatina
(Bellini); Norma Tarzetta (Bellini.)"

The names of the contributing artists were not giv-
en. The price of admission however was specified at $3 per
seat.

FREE LUNCH TO PATRONS

In this access of zeal to supply the aesthetic
tastes of their patrons, their gastronomic wants were not
overlooked by the versatile proprietors of these establishments. Besides furnishing the choicest wines and liquors and
a copious free lunch at the bar, many a menu boasted of culi-
nary specialities to please the most exacting gourmet of the
day. The El Dorado was first to serve chicken in the shell,
a delicious dish concocted of butter, cream, eggs, white meat
of chicken and sherry, lightly blended and served in shells.

Of all the early gambling resorts that remained
throughout the greater part of the existence of the Barbary
Coast, the Bella Union at Washington and Kearny Streets, generally ribald, always entertaining, proved the most adaptable
to the changing and capricious moods of the populace. De-
spite its destruction several times by the great fires that
ravaged the city from 1849 through 1851, and the many changes
in its management, the Bella Union maintained a continuous
existence for almost sixty years, during the greater part of
which it operated as a so-called melodeon or concert saloon,
in reality a low-class variety or music-hall, playing to men
only, occasionally with an ambitious performance, but usually

pandering to the coarse and vulgar. At intervals it occupied
a place as family theatre presenting melodrama at fifty cents
top admission.

In its later years it was called successively the
Haymarket Theatre and the Imperial Concert Hall, finally end-
ing its days as the Eden Musee housing a penny arcade and a
waxworks exhibit.

MELODEONS AND MUSIC HALLS

The melodeons had no dance floors, offering only
liquor and theatrical diversion. They were so called, because
when first introduced in San Francisco each was equipped with
the musical instrument of that name. It was a small reed organ worked by treadles acting upon a suction bellows, the air
being drawn in through the reeds.

In time however, the word became the common desig-
nation of a type of resort which offered entertainment for men
only, no women being permitted to enter except the performers
and waitresses. A few catered principally to Mexicans and
Negroes, tempering the entertainment accordingly.

The Bella Union, the Olympic, the Pacific, Bert's
New Idea Melodeon, the Adelphi and Gilbert's Melodeon topped
the list of this type of amusement house. Indeed, many who
appeared at the Bella Union and other Barbary Coast Melodeons
became in later years outstanding dramatic, vaudeville and
musical comedy stars.

The converse was also true. Popular favorites, among them the celebrated Madam Eliza Biscaccianti, known the world over as the "American Thrush," succumbing to the innumerable temptations besetting them on all sides, presented their broken bodies and reputations at the doors of the Bella Union and like establishments, begging the chance to market the poor remnants of their once famous talents.

> "Pacific Street from the waterfront westward to Kearny Street and beyond, was a solid mass of dance-halls, melodeons, cheap groggeries, wine and beer dens, which were popularly known as deadfalls; and concert saloons which offered both dancing and entertainment, most of them in cellars." [1]

Usually in the cheaper resorts, the sole musical instrument was a piano as out of tune as the room that housed it, occasionally supplemented by a squeaky fiddle or blaring trombone or clarinet.

The melodeons of this class were like the dance-halls and concert saloons except that they had no facilities for dancing. They offered only liquor and theatrical diversion.

> "Many similar resorts were in operation on Montgomery, Kearny and Stockton Streets and on other thoroughfares within the confines of the Barbary Coast, while the northern limits of the quarter were marked by a row of Mexican fandango houses on Broadway opposite the County Jail." [1]

In these last named places, which were particularly disreputable, the principal musical instrument was the guitar and the favorite dance, a very daring version of the fandango.

---

1 Asbury, Herbert. _Barbary Coast_ (New York: Alfred Knopf, 1933.)

From late afternoon until dawn all of the dives
were thronged with a motley crew of murderers, thieves, bur-
glars, gamblers and degenerates of every description. Every
known vice and crime was common to these haunts.

TERRIFIC STREET

The Chinese gambling resorts which by the latter
half of 1854 lined the upper end of Sacramento Street and
the greater part of Grant Avenue, were in the early days
small and meanly furnished. But even then, according to
Soule's Annals:

> "At the innermost end of some of the principal
> gambling places, there was an orchestra of five
> or six native musicians, who produced such ex-
> traordinary sounds from their curiously shaped
> instruments as severely tortured the white men
> to listen to. Occasionally a songster added his
> howl or shriek to the excruciating harmony....

> "In later times the Barbary Coast meant only the
> single block on Pacific Street between Kearny
> and Montgomery Streets, a short stretch of dan-
> gerous and disreputable thoroughfare, which was
> also widely known, after the middle eighteen-
> nineties, as Terrific Street.

> "But originally, and until the Coast was devast-
> ated by the earthquake and fire of 1906, the
> term was applied to the entire area, including
> the red light district, wherein criminals and
> prostitutes congregated. Roughly it occupied a
> greater or lesser portion of the territory
> bounded on the east by the waterfront and East
> Street, now the Embarcadero; on the South by
> Clay and Commercial Streets; on the West by Grant
> Avenue and Chinatown; and on the North by Broad-
> way with occasional overflows into the region
> around North Beach and Telegraph Hill.

"During most of the long period in which the
Barbary Coast was almost the universal synonym
for debauchery, its most iniquitous features were
confined within the rectangular district limited
by Broadway and Washington, Montgomery and
Stockton Streets...." 1

In the noisome passages and alleys, offshoots of
this district, as well as in the main thoroughfares from
which they sprouted, were to be found what the San Francisco
Call on November 28, 1869 described as "scenes of wretchedness
and pollution unparalleled on this side of the great moun-
tains."

Not until February, 1917, did the Barbary Coast establishments fold up their tents, yielding to the clamor of
outraged public opinion, and the resultant legislation that
drove them from their doors. 2

The ravages and pillage of organized bands of gang-
sters, arsonists and murderers going variously under the names
of the Hounds, Rangers, Sidney Ducks and Hoodlums were sub-
dued by Committees of Vigilance. And while at first the attempts at regulatory legislation failed to break the grip of
commercialized vice upon the city, eventually, through the
unceasing efforts of various clerical and lay reformers, Barbary Coast after nearly seventy years of inglorious living,
faded into the limbo of nearly forgotten things. Today, the
few short streets in North Beach are dead and deserted, a ghost
town within the throbbing city.

---

1 Soule, Frank. Annals of San Francisco (San Francisco:
Gihon, John H. M. D. James Nisbet, Pub., Montgomery Street.)
2 Feb. 14, 1917--police blockade: by midnight, red light
district deserted. Feb. 16, 1917--further closure, and within week, all had abandoned the Coast.

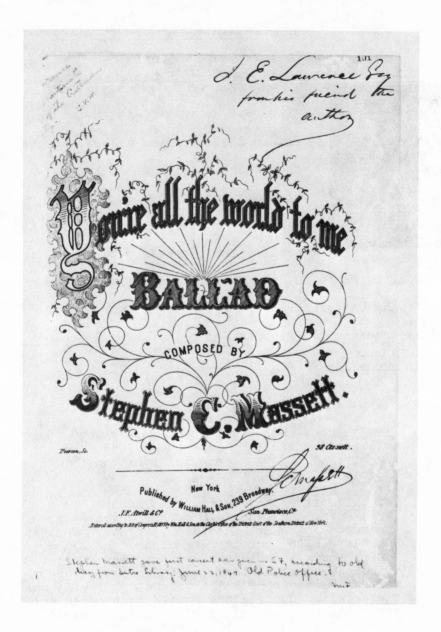

CHAPTER FOUR: FESTIVALS, FIREMEN'S BALLS

 century ago, in May of 1836,   Mr. Jacob
Primer Leese arrived at Yerba Buena with
the intention of establishing a mercantile
business and was granted a small parcel of
land at the intersection of Clay and Dupont (Grant) Streets. He began erecting
his dwelling there on July First, and construction was hastened
so that the building was completed on the morning of the Fourth
of July, causing two reasons for celebration. Soule's Annals
of San Francisco reported it as follows:

THE FIRST SOCIAL FUNCTION OF IMPORTANCE

"Two events--each great in their way were to be
celebrated. First, Independence Day, and next
the arrival of Mr. Leese in the country, his
welcome, and house warming.

"At this time there was lying in the cove of
Yerba Buena the American barque "Don Quixote"
commanded by   Mr. Leese's partner Captain
Hinckley--also another American ship and a
Mexican brig. These vessels supplied every bit
of colored bunting they could furnish to decor-
ate Mr. Leese's hall. A splendid display was
the result. Outside the building floated ami-
cably the Mexican and American flags--the first
time the latter was displayed on the shore of
Yerba Buena.

"Captain Hinckley seems to have been somewhat
extravagant in his passion for sweet sounds,
since he always travelled with a band of music
in his train. Through this cause the most
stylish orchestra, perhaps ever before heard in
California, was provided by him. This consisted
of a clarinet, flute, violin, drum, fife and
bugle; besides two small six-pounders to form
the bass, and to add their emphatic roar to the
swelling din, when a toast of more than usual
importance should be given.

"The feast was prepared, the minstrels were met
and the guests began to assemble about three
o'clock on the afternoon of the Fourth. They
were about sixty in number and included General
M. G. Vallejo and all the principal families
from the neighborhood of Sonoma such as the
Castros, Martinez, etc., as well as the chief
inhabitants of Yerba Buena. At five o'clock
the dinner was served.

"The guests were as happy as mortals could well
be. All went 'merry as a marriage bell'--at
ten o'clock dancing and other amusements commenced and the ball was kept hot rolling in-
cessantly all that night and the following day.
For as Mr. Leese naively observes in his highly
interesting and amusing diary 'Our Fourth ended
on the evening of the Fifth.'" 1

Records give meagre information regarding particular
social affairs before 1840; probably the first inhabitants
of the pueblo were eager to celebrate with music, dancing,
and song on the slightest provocation. The arrival of people such as Commodore Stockton, who came in July of 1846, or
events such as the re-christening of Yerba Buena as San Francisco were especially memorable.

---

1 Soule, Frank. _Annals of San Francisco_ (New York: D. Appleton Co., 1854.)

CHARACTERISTICS OF EARLY SOCIAL LIFE

Society of the Gold Rush era, free and cordial, ready to give a friendly reception to a stranger, was unique. It looked upon the newcomer with favor; nobody cared whether he belonged to a distinguished family, had moved in fashionable circles or possessed wealth or influential friends. "Is he or she well educated, talented, or entertaining?" they asked. Singers or instrumentalists, virtuosi or talented amateurs got a hearty welcome, became popular instantly, and often were given the opportunity to earn what seems to us large sums of money. Albert Benard de Russailh in his Last Adventure remarked:

> "A musician could earn two ounces ($32) by scraping a squeaky fiddle for two hours every evening or by puffing into an asthmatic flute." 1

Stephen C. Massett is a notable example of a newcomer who found musical talent advantageous in the new city. Massett, -- singer, composer, actor and self-styled "rolling stone" arrived unheralded and seeking a "change of fortune." He had been here hardly a month or two when he gave what is described as having been "the first entertainment in San Francisco" on June 22, 1849, an event to which most everyone sought admission. Through this and later efforts he became a memorable figure among the pioneers and in time accumulated a sizeable fortune. 2

---

1 de Russailh, Albert B. Last Adventure 1851 (San Francisco: Westgate Press, 1931.)
2 See Steve Massett, Vol. 1, S. F. Theatre Research Project, O.P. 465-03-286.

Living accomodations were lamentably poor during the first few years following the discovery of gold; comforts were few, crude and expensive but as the population increased and social life blossomed, the mode of living of San Franciscans was luxurious. Everybody wanted and most everyone had a neat house, elegant table-ware, fine furniture, Brussels carpets, and other accoutrements of fine living. Many of the lesser mechanics and even common laborers had fine homes. In every occupation men became rich; stingy men and misers were rare. Another unique trait of early community life was that although many of the people possessed the equipment required for entertaining privately -- social life of the Gold Rush era was definitely more public than private. Mr. John P. Young states:

> "The decade of the Fifties had nearly closed before any sign was witnessed of a tendency to form social groups." 1

THE RIGHT ARM OF THE CITY

Oddly enough, the firemen of the city formed the first social group and were leaders in pioneer community life. Fire was a tremendous hazard, consequently volunteer fire brigades were organized. They were like clubs and men of character deemed it a civic duty to belong to one. Mr. Young says:

> "The enthusiastic praise of the writer of the 'Annals' was doubtless deserved by the fire brigade, which he informs us was regarded as

---

1 Young, John P. San Francisco, A History of the Pacific Coast Metropolis (San Francisco: The S. J. Clarke Pub. Co.)

> 'the right arm of San Francisco.' They were
> the elite of the city and considered it an
> honor to belong to a company. The Sansome Com-
> pany's building cost $24,000, and was furnished
> as well as any residence in the city. It
> boasted 'a large library.' The Fifties were
> remarkable for the interest taken by people in
> parades and public celebrations of all sorts
> and in no American City was there a greater de-
> sire shown for such diversion than in San Fran-
> cisco. No event or anniversary of consequence
> was allowed to pass without a demonstration and
> in these outpourings the firemen with their ap-
> paratus were the most conspicuous feature."

The firemen of the Fifties were doubtless worthy of strong praise and early newspapers such as the Wide West devoted much space to their social and civic activities. Apparently several of the fire companies had bands of excellent musical quality and on occasion made journeys to Sacramento, Marysville, and other communities. (For Fire Depts., see Appendix B.)

FIRST DANCE ORCHESTRAS

Dancing was an extremely popular form of entertainment and recreation in gold rush days. Mr. John S. Hittel, author of Resources of California states:

> "Dancing is almost universal. The children of
> every school in our chief city must have pic-
> nics and dances in May and at Christmas. The
> climate along the coast is peculiarly favorable
> to dancing, for as the evenings and nights are
> cold, it is as pleasant to dance in summer as
> in winter."

Music for dancing was provided by a variety of bands and orchestras. For the large and more formal functions "a full band of good music" was employed. For less pompous affairs, orchestras of every description were engaged. Beginning with a lone concertino, dance music was furnished by violin and guitar duos, trios of piano, violin, and flute, and larger groups of most every size and instrumentation. Of one such orchestra, Albert Benard de Russailh remarked as follows:

> "The music is fairly good and is certainly noisy. Eight or ten passable musicians play all the popular dance tunes for quadrilles, waltzes, and polkas."

The latter were the most popular dances; other types of dances enjoyed at this time were cotillions, mazourkas, gallopades, and marches. An insight into the extremely cosmopolitan membership of the early orchestral groups is given in the following amusing news item. It was reported by Mr. Stephen C. Massett and is recorded in the California Historical Quarterly. (Vol. 15, p. 45):

> "The Englishman insisted that 'Rule Brittania' was the greatest air out; this fired up a Yankee who insisted upon playing nothing else but 'Hail Columbia' or for a slight variation 'Yandee Doodle.' The Frenchman could not stand this at all, saying 'Zat de Merikans have not tune but see Nigger Hairs,' and 'Zat he vood play nosink but see musique of La Belle France.' All this time a Hungarian exile was amusing himself by sending forth a solitary Polka from a dismal flageolette, to the no small discomforture of the plump-faced German (the director) who--running from the scene of action exclaimed: 'Mein Gott! Vat a country! Vat a peoples!'"

A TYPICAL MASK-BALL

Balls were given with amazing frequency and averaged several each week throughout the year. Taking place with

such regularity, and being considered such an ordinary part
of life, detailed descriptions of their attendance and procedure are rare in the writings of early chroniclers.

A Ball celebrating the Admission of California to
the Union was held on October 29, 1850. It is described in
the Annals of San Francisco as follows:

> "Some five hundred gentlemen and three hundred
> ladies met at the grandest public ball that had
> yet been witnessed in the city, and danced and
> made merry till daylight, in the pride and joy
> of their hearts that California was truly now
> the thirty-first state of the Union."

Mask balls and fancy dress balls were very popular.
Soule says:

> "By the private entrance come the maskers, male
> and female. The Spanish bandit, with his high
> tapering hat, ornamented with ribbons; the gypsy,
> with her basket and cards; the Bloomer, bounti-
> ful in short skirts and satin-covered extremi-
> ties, the ardent young militaire, with a borrowed
> uniform and sparse moustache, which requires,
> like bees, the assistance of a clattering tin
> kettle to congregate the scattered portions; the
> Swiss ballad-singers, with their hurdy-gurdy and
> tambourine; the faunting Cyprian, not veiled by
> domino or mask; and the curious but respectable
> lady, hidden by cloak and false visage. There
> is the Frenchman in a fantastical dress; a Galli
> Count imitating the Yankee affecting 'Aunty
> Vermont' and men already feeling the force of
> their libations, affecting sobriety.
>
> "Now the band commences, the bow is drawn, the
> breath blown and domino and mask are whisked
> about into the midst of the dizzy maze by the
> Turk who has forgotten his cimeter; the Pole
> who has nothing of Koscuisco or Poniatowski ex-
> cept the tall cap et cetera; the Vermonter imi-
> tating a courtier of Charles II and a Red Repub-
> lican affecting Silsbee or Dan Marble. Away
> they whirl through the waltz, or dash along the
> mazourka, or crash promiscuously in the gallo-
> pade. Where there are no masks, exercise brings
> no new rose tint or crimson to the soft cheek--
> the rouge or carmine is too thick for that.

"The music draws to a close and ends with a
grand flourish. The potations begin to oper-
ate, the violent seek recontres, old scores
are to be settled and new quarrels commenced.
Jealousy's eyes take a greener tinge from the
bottle imp and woman, forgetting her preroga-
tive--gentleness--joins the ring and gives point
to feminine oaths by the use of feminine nails.
Gradually the room is thinned, the first depart-
ing being careful to select the finest umbrellas.
And when daylight comes it finds the usual char-
acteristics of such 'Banquet Hall deserted.'
Such is a slight description of the 'California
Exchange' in the height of its ball day glories,
where--in one night thousands of dollars were
taken in for tickets and thousands at the bar
for drinks. Amen."

It was customary in the Fifties to give public
Balls as benefits for people who were ill or in financial
distress. Advertisements and new stories such as this for
the Wide West March 21, 1858, were common:

"A Ball for the benefit of John O'Brien, came
off at Assembly Hall on the evening of the 17th.
We learned that the affair passed off most
pleasantly and hope that the receipts will suffice to secure the proposed relief."

SOIREES AND CONCERTS

Another style of entertainment enjoyed by the pioneers was the soirée: concert and ball. These affairs were
probably introduced by the early British residents as this
type of social gathering is still much in vogue in England
and Scotland. The soirée usually commenced with a musical
program, vocal or instrumental. Often the entire audience
joined in singing favorite songs much in the manner of modern community singing. The performers might also include

other entertainers such as magicians, gymnasts, orators and dramatists. The program concluded with a ball and everyone joined in the dancing.

These were lively affairs and in the following notice, one cannot help but note the promise, made by the sponsors, to keep the conduct of those attending the soirée above reproach. This appeared in the <u>Wide West</u> April 27, 1857:

> "On the evening of April 30th, a May Day Soirée is to be given by the Pennsylvania Engine Co. at the Mechanic's Institute Pavilion, combining a Concert and Ball. The Misses Mandeville will sing several of their popular songs and a full orchestra discourse eloquent music. Everything is to be conducted in such a manner as to render this one of the most attractive entertainments imaginable. The entire Company will give their personal attention to the object of preventing the slightest contretemps, or impropriety in the character of those present on this occasion."

CHIEF HOTELS

As there was but little strictly private entertainment most social functions were held at the various hotels, resorts and halls. Many of the most prominent people resided in hotels and there the gentle-folk gathered to entertain or to be entertained. People met in hotels daily to discuss the affairs of the day, dine and perhaps set out upon their favorite social diversions. (For Hotels, See Appendix A.)

Unfortunately, the hotels were repeatedly destroyed by fire; some were rebuilt, enlarged and equipped more sumptuously than ever; others were only repaired and became somewhat degraded.

Popular restaurants of this era included Delmonicos, the Sutter House, Irving House, Jackson House, Franklin House, and the Lafayette House. The Fountain Head and Winn's Branch, operated by Mr. M. L. Winn, were quite ostentatious; they were distinguished because of the proprietor's refusal to permit the use of alcoholic beverages.

Russ' Gardens was a resort located in the suburbs between the Mission Road and the Beach. This was a favorite rendezvous and the scene of many festivals, concerts and other carnival-like doings.

About 1854, a large music hall was built in Bush Street near Montgomery Street by the adventurous Mr. Henry Meiggs. The more quiet folk of the city were entertained there with concerts, oratorios, lectures, fairs and the like.

PARADES AND MAY DAY FESTIVALS

Parades were another very important part of pioneer social life, much more interest being shown in them than in present times. Often the entire population turned out to witness or take part in a procession and the burial rites honoring the passing of a prominent citizen. On such occasions bands with muffled instruments marched through the streets playing dirges and funeral marches.

On commemorative occasions such as Admission Day and the Fourth of July, a parade was the outstanding feature of the celebration. More emphasis was given to the observance of Washington's Birthday than at present for in addition to the closing of financial and business houses a mammoth parade and oratory were the order of the day.

May Day was celebrated with an annual festival held by the Turner Gesang Verein. These festivals, often of two or three days duration, included concerts, oration and song, dancing and gymnastic exercises. Between five and six thousand Germans resided in San Francisco by 1854 and from these chiefly came the professional musicians of the city.

March 17 was also a gala day when the ten thousand or more Irish citizens celebrated in honor of Saint Patrick. They were usually joined by the people of all nationalities including the Chinese who were numerous, well-liked and well-behaved. Anti-Oriental prejudice was fostered in a later era when the demand for cheap labor became urgent.

OTHER DIVERSIONS

Steamer Day was an event of more than passing interest to the pioneers. Crowds gathered to meet the Eastern or Panama boats and much social activity was usually attendant upon the arrival of relatives and friends.

Picnics and excursions to outlying resorts, gambling, horse racing, and billiards were popular pastimes. From 1849 to 1852 bear-baiting and a modified form of Spanish bull-fighting took place at Mission Dolores. Historians do not mention it, but presumably there were bands present at these events.

Early San Franciscans had a profound love for the music of the theatre, opera, church choir and the minstrel. They had an almost fanatical devotion to the stars of these; attendance at some musical function or amusement was their chief diversion and played an important part in pioneer social life.

CHAPTER FIVE: CHURCH CHOIRS

hough the niceties of religion were some-
what alien to the anarchistic struggle for
gold that so characterized early San Francisco, when a parson appeared   late   in
1848 he was made welcome.   The man, Reverend T. Dwight Hunt, a Congregationalist,
arrived from the Hawaiian Islands on October 29, 1848;   the
next day he was invited by the citizens, at a mass   meeting
held in Portsmouth Square for that purpose to act   as   the
city's chaplain.   He was appointed for one year, at a   salary
of $2,000, and held services twice each Sunday at the school-
house in the Plaza. This was over three-quarters of a ·cen-
tury after Mission Dolores dedication.

Reverend Hunt was the first Protestant clergyman,
located as such, in the state of California, although there
is record of a Methodist sermon given in an adobe building
opposite Portsmouth Square on April 24, 1847, and still earlier of sea captains who sometimes "spoke the word."

Perhaps the most colorful of the early ministers
was the Reverend William Taylor, a Methodist, who on December 3, 1849, went to the Plaza to conduct an open air service. In his autobiography, Seven Years of Street Preaching,

he tells about it thus:

> "Now, should a poor preacher presume to go into
> their midst, and interfere with their business,
> by thrilling every house with the songs of Zion
> and the peals of Gospel Truth,he would be like-
> ly to wake up the lion in his lair...I selected
> for my pulpit a carpenter's bench, which stood
> in front of one of the largest gambling houses
> in the city. I got Mrs. Taylor and another lady
> or two comfortably seated,in the care of a good
> brother, and taking the stand, I sung in a high
> key, 'Hear the royal proclamation, the glad ti-
> dings of Salvation, etc.'

> "On Sunday afternoon, the 5th of May, 1850, I
> took my stand upon the porch of the 'Old Adobe,'
> on the Plaza, and after singing up a crowd of
> about a thousand persons, I announced my text."

Music in the Protestant Churches thus began most
humbly and in a purely democratic manner. The songs of religion were taken to the people, wherever a crowd could be gathered. The Salvation Army was thus foreshadowed by street
preachers who planted themselves before saloons, and their
words and singing blended with the rattle of chips in the
gambling halls. Here was heard 'The Chariot, the Chariot,
It's Wheels Roll in Fire,' and many other hymns.

THE EARLIEST TABERNACLES

The first Protestant church, organized as such, was
the Presbyterian Church under the guidance of Reverend Albert
Williams who called his flock of six persons together in a
tent on Dupont Street, May 20, 1849. The first Protestant
church building in San Francisco and in California was built
by the Baptists who organized in June, 1849, and   dedicated
their church in August of that year with the Reverend Osgood

C. Wheeler as pastor. This church, constructed of Oregon pine
boards for walls and ship's sails spread over scantlings for
a roof, was located on the north side of Washington   Street
near Stockton.

The Presbyterians, later in the year, erected a
church building that had been bought in New York, dismantled,
and shipped to San Francisco by way of the Horn. At its dedication there were thirty-two ladies present, the largest assembly to date of that sex. Most pretentious of the '49
churches was the Grace Episcopal which was dedicated December
30th. This wooden structure on the corner of Powell and Hohn
Streets, measured twenty by sixty feet, with a belfry in which
swung an eight hundred pound bell.

At the time of the Gold Rush there were two Catholic churches in the city, but neither was active as a place
of worship. The Mission Dolores, very poor due to a theft of
its funds, had been secularized since 1834 by a Mexican de-
cree, and the little adobe church of St. Francis was in an
uninviting and apathetic state. Catholic services were resumed in June of 1851 after the arrival of Bishop Alamany..
The first church to be built was St. Patrick's, on the site
of the Palace Hotel, while the Mission Dolores and the St.
Francis on Pacific Street were reopened as places of worship.

The cornerstone of 'Old St. Mary's,' which still
stands on the corner of California Street and Grant Avenue,

was laid   July 17, 1853.   This church was   built at a cost of $175,000 and remained for many years the most imposing relig-ious structure in the city.

By the end of the 1850's practically every denomin-ation was   represented by one or   more churches,   there being thirteen Protestant   churches, seven   Catholic, two   Jewish, three Negro, and   Unitarian, Swedenborgian, and   Chinese, one each.   (See Appendix C.)

The earlier churches were very informal in the con-duct of their services,   and unison singing by the congrega-tion was the accepted custom.   'Old Hundred' was a particular favorite.   Attracted by the lavish sums paid to entertainers, the city had become a   mecca for good musicians   and singers. These found their   way into the   churches and their   superior voices soon inaugurated the choir system.

Every church   had its choir, and the quartet   choir was particularly   fashionable.   Leaders of   these choirs were generally   excellent musicians whose   names also appeared   in many other places as members of   the symphonic and choral so-cieties.   Among the better known were Mr. Theodore Smith, or-ganist at St. John's;   Professor George F. Pellinos, organist at   Calvary Presbyterian;   Monsieur Planel,   organist at   Our Lady of the Victories;   R. Herold, organist at   Church of the Advent;   Messers. Elliot, Zander, Titcomb, G.T. Evans, and S. A. Hastings.

SACRED CONCERTS

Special benefit concerts of sacred music formed a large part of the musical activities in the churches. These were usually given to raise funds to liquidate debts on the buildings, a process which often had to be repeated due to the frequent incendiary fires which leveled a large portion of the city.

The best of these benefit performances were the three given in 1852 at the Grace Episcopal Church by Signora Elisa Biscaccianti, one of the most famous singers in the early musical history of San Francisco. It was she who sang Rossini's "Stabat Mater," the first oratorio to be heard here. This was indeed a great event and proved to be highly successful both artistically and financially. Signora Biscaccianti, more than any other person perhaps, provided the stimulus to the appreciation of good music in San Francisco.

Innumerable other church benefits and sacred concerts followed throughout the 1850's. At the Unitarian Church, February 23, 1857, the quartet choir, with Mrs. Oliphant as soloist, gave the "Oratorio of Elijah." The "Mass of Charon," sung by French artists under the direction of M. Planel, signalized the dedication of the French Church, Our Lady of the Victories. The review of another such concert is quoted from the San Francisco Bulletin of February 27, 1856:

> "The concert of sacred music last night, at the First Congregational Church, was well attended. The compositions of Handel, Haydn, and Rossini

were given with much effect, and delighted every one present. The amateur performers have every reason to be gratified at the success of their first concert...The association of amateur singers is composed of Mr. Shattuck, Mrs. Scribner, Mrs. Titcomb, Misses Merrill and Bartlett, and Messers. Zander, Titcomb, Elliott, Pearson, Olney and Scadder...The proceeds were devoted to the Mariner's Church, on Clark Street, placing the church entirely out of debt."

SEMI-SECULAR PROGRAMS

In addition to the sacred music concerts by the choirs there were many other types of musical programs given in the churches. Operatic and semi-popular numbers were often interspersed between oratorio selections in order to liven up the program. At a grand sacred concert for the benefit of the Church of the Advent the program also included the Wedding March from "Mid-Summer Night's Dream," selections from Mozart's "Don Juan," and the overture to "Der Windschütz." This affair was especially successful because it was directed by Herold whose choir was reputedly one of the best in the city. (See Chapter 12.)

Musicians were often invited by the churches to render special selections during services. A favorite was Mr. Lapfgeer whose French horn solos were enjoyed by many congregations. It is also noted in the pages of the San Francisco Bulletin that the leading singers of one church often appeared as guest artists in some other church. Nowhere has any word been found to indicate that the choir members were paid for their services, and it is therefore safe to assume that the choristers offered their good offices gratis.

The organists, who usually were the choir-masters as well, were paid of course. A reviewer, "100," of the San Francisco Bulletin, mentions that Mr. G. T. Evans, of Calvary Presbyterian Church, was the best paid organist in the city. This church also possessed the largest and best organ on the Pacific Coast. Built by Henry Erben of New York, it had forty-six stops, over two thousand pipes, and was installed at a cost of $8,000.

REVIEWS BY "100"

A series of interesting articles about the churches of the city appear in the San Francisco Bulletin during 1856. The writer signed himself "100" because "Old Hundred" was his favorite hymn. A few of his pertinent remarks are quoted:

July 8th:

> "The First Presbyterian Church has a choir of ten instead of the fashionable quartet so much in vogue in other churches. As a consequence nearly the whole congregation joined in singing the old-fashioned hymns."

August 5th:

> "St. Mary's: 'A small, plain organ evidently not intended for the finished church furnished the music...The singing, while good for church music, was not as fine as we have heard at an Opera House, though frequently closely approaching it in the style, execution, and manners of the choristers.'"

October 6th:

> "Methodist Episcopal: 'The church has a large choir, and a sweet toned melodeon...There never appeared to be any rivalry between the organist and the singers, as to which could secure the largest share of the admiration and attention of the audience.'"

August 11th:

> "Negro Zion Church: 'The choir singing, which
> was excellent even if somewhat untrained, was
> led by an individual who sat behind the stove
> and appeared to have no music.'"

All in all, church choirs played a **considerable**
part toward inculcating a love of good music in San Francisco.

CHAPTER SIX: EARLY CHORAL SOCIETIES

uring the 1850's music in San Francisco was largely dominated by the German peoples who had immigrated to America in large numbers and pushed on to California. They were a music loving people who firmly adhered to the associations and pleasures of their youth beside the Rhine and Vistula.

As early as 1853 there were four German societies devoted to music, and the following year the Turner Gesang Verein (Gymnastic Musical Association) was estimated by Young, in his History of San Francisco, to number 6,000 persons.

GENESIS IN ANCIENT GUILDS

Among the German groups, singing has been a part of their lives for some centuries, with its beginning in the various craftsmen's guilds during the Middle Ages. From among its members each guild had its gymnastic team, its actor's group and choral club which vied with similar groups in the other guilds. At the annual fairs the guilds exhibited their industrial arts and cultural accomplishments, with prizes awarded to the best shoemaker, the best choral club, etc. Wagner has immortalized these competitive songfests of the guilds in his opera Die Meistersinger.

An outgrowth of the earlier guilds were the Verein, societies which dropped the industrial activities and became social and political organizations. The origin of the May Day Festivals, as sponsored by the Vereins, was a political one with roots in the fatherland. This celebration, important among Germans everywhere, has the same significance as our own Fourth of July.

THE TURNVEREINS

The Turnverein associations, which existed in America in nearly all large cities, were simply social societies which cultivated physical culture and choral singing. In Germany, however, they were also political organizations that dated back to Napoleonic days. The "Little Corporal" had conquered Germany and the desire to repulse him was general, but no hope of immediate resistance existed. A patriot named Doctor Jahn conceived the idea of establishing gymnasia, for two reasons -- to prepare young men for a future war against France, and to instill patriotic ardor for a movement designed to make a united Germany. Jahn established the first Turnplatz, or gymnasium, near Berlin in 1811. After the Peace of Paris was concluded, the princes of the various little kingdoms broke their solemn promises of political reform, and the government, suspicious of the gymnasia, ordered them closed. But the spirit of republicanism could not be eradicated, and revolutions were rife during 1830 and again in 1848.

After the revolution of May in 1848 and the failure of the Constitutional Convention to draft a constitution that would unite the thirty-six little despotic principalities under a single liberal government in which the people would have a representative voice, the ultra conservative Diet of Junkers again won supremacy and everywhere the liberals were persecuted. Tens of thousands fled the country, most of them to America. As all political organizations were again banned, the work of liberalism was carried on under cover of the gymnastic and singing clubs, called the Turner and Gesang Vereins. These societies, now mainly social, were set up anew as soon as the Germans reached America, the first being instituted by a pupil of Jahn, Doctor Beck, at Northhampton, Massachussetts, in 1825.

THE FATHER OF LOCAL CHORALES

In 1851 Dr. Augustus H. Malech, who has been called the father of San Francisco music, arrived here from the East, having originally come from Veide, Germany, to fill a New York engagement with Jenny Lind. Here, it is said, he started the first German singing society, "Die Sänger Am Stillen Meer," and, with his wife, a soprano, gave concerts. Out of his singing society eventually grew the Mannerchor and Sängerbund societies.

The activities of two other early organizations are described in the Daily Herald of June 2nd, 1852, and April 30th, 1853:

"The Alleghanians. The concert of the Alleghanians last evening at Grace Church was very
respectfully and fully attended, and the singing
was heard to much better advantage than at the
theatre. They sang several of their best selections and were encored, and on the whole the
entertainment was one of the most successful of
the series. The next concert will be given at
the Adelphi Theatre on Thursday evening."

"Aeolian Vocalists. The Aeolian Vocalists, composed of one lady and four gentlemen, will give
their first grand concert (after the style of
the Alleghanians) Saturday evening, April 30,
1853, at Armory Hall. Professor O. Sutro will
preside at the Pianoforte."

The first musical organization to assume an outstanding place in the city was the San Francisco Philharmonic
Society which had gotten well under way by the end of 1852.
Henry Meiggs was the first president, and the musical direct-
or, George Loder, was very active in music circles. This
group was composed of the best musicians and amateur singers
in the city at that time. This announcement appears in the
Daily Herald of July 17, 1853:

"Ladies and Gentlemen of the Philharmonic Society, and such other readers of Music as are de-
sirous of meeting for practice,are respectfully
invited to attend the First rehearsal, under
the direction of Mr. George Loder, at the Pine
Street Baptist Church, on Tuesday evening, July
19, at 7:30 o'clock."

PACIFIC MUSICAL TROUPE

An early triumph of the Philharmonic Society occurred in July, 1853, in conjunction with the Pacific Musical
Troupe, at the first concert in the new Musical Hall. This
troupe, for whom the hall was built, was a quartet composed

of Mrs. Laura Jones, soprano, Miss Maria Leach, contralto, Mr. J. Beutler, tenor, and Mr. J. Connor Smith, basso. Musical Hall on Bush Street near Montgomery, seated twelve hundred persons and was by far the most comfortable auditorium in the city. A review in the Daily Herald, July 27, 1853, is quoted in part:

> "They opened with a beautiful quartette entitled 'A Greeting to California'...The selections were excellent, comprising every variety of English music, Quartette, Duett, Solo, Ballad, Glee, Madrigal, Song and Chorus...A portion of the Philharmonic Society, consisting of about forty members, appeared in chorus. They sang with spirit and with scarcely a jar..."

Other numbers included: "Here in Cool Grot," a quartette; "Crowned with a Tempest," basso solo assisted by the chorus and orchestra; "Blow Gentle Gates," quartette; "Hark! Smiling Morn," a glee; "The Hunter," duett; "Down in the Flowery Vale," a madrigal; "I'm Going for a Soldier, Jenny," a solo; and "We Met by Chance," a song. This combination of talents proved most popular for two years, during which time McCabe's Journal lists fourteen such concerts.

A later concert of these two groups is reported by Jeems Pipes of Pipesville (non-de-plume of Stephen Massett) in "Chit Chat" from the Pioneer Monthly Magazine of January 1854:

> "We must at least make mention of the fact that Hayden's (sic) 'Oratorio of the Seasons' has been produced at Musical Hall; Mrs. L. A. Jones and Messrs. Buetler and Smith taking the leading parts, and the Philharmonic Society, assisted by Miss Maria Leach, singing the choruses. It was indeed a rich musical treat, and all concerned are deserving of high praise."

A COLLECTIVE CONCERT

A second series of concerts by these two groups was even more successful due to the appearance of Miska Hauser, the famous violinist. The Daily Herald of October 21,22, 23, 1853, reports it thus:

"The Troupe proper were assisted by a very good chorus from the members of the Philharmonic Society, and by Miska Hauser, the violinist; Mr. Herold, the pianist, and Mr. Hildebrand, a performer on the violoncello. The duet from 'Linda di Chamounix' was sung with much taste and spirit by Mrs. Jones and Mr. Buetler, Miska Hauser's execution of the 'Rondo de Concerto,' induced an encore, to which he responded with the 'Carnival of Venice,' and he never in our hearing played it more effectively. Miss Leach was also encored in the song of the 'Minstrel Boy.'"

"Last evening the second of the second series of concerts by the Pacific Musical Troupe was given before the fullest House we have yet seen in attendance at these entertainments. In addition to the members of the company, Madame La Reintree appeared and sang the sweet song of 'John Anderson, my Jo' with an effect that caused an encore. The ballad solos by Mrs. Jones and Miss Leach; the violin solo by Miska Hauser; the quartette and the choruses were also rendered in a manner highly creditable to the performers."

"The third concert of the Pacific Musical Troupe was enjoyed last evening by an audience that filled this spacious Hall. That ever-pleasing song 'The Last Rose of Summer' arranged as a quartette, was very sweetly sung by the Troupe. Mrs. Jones sang 'The Gondolier,' which has become quite a favorite. The violin solo, 'Souvenir de Donizetti,' was executed by Miska Hauser in a manner that elicited an encore, to which he responded with the equally pleasing strains of 'Kathleen Mavourneen.' The other performers acquitted themselves very creditably, and the audience manifested their pleasure by frequent applause."

THE HARMONIE AND PHILHARMONIC

Perhaps the most active man in music circles during the 50's was Mr. Rudolph Herold, organist, orchestra leader, and director of the San Francisco Harmonie, organized August 27, 1854, Germania Philharmonic, 1855, Harmonic Society, January, 1857, and the Cecilien Verein, October 29,   1859. Throughout the decade scores of reviews of musical events are full of praise for his work with orchestras and choral groups. He was the outstanding man of those years.

Of these societies the Germania and Harmonie were predominately German organizations, while the Harmonie and the old San Francisco Philharmonic were American.   The Harmonic Society, composed of eighty-five members, mostly amateurs, was one of the most successful in the city. Two criticisms of their work appear in Wide West of November 22, 1857, and February 14, 1858, respectively:

> "We are certain that general satisfaction would
> be produced if a concert were occasionally given
> where operatic selections predominate. Such mu-
> sic as that of 'The Creation' and 'The Seasons'
> is a little 'heavy' to be kept up for a couple
> of hours..."

> "A large audience was assembled at Musical Hall.
> The first part of the concert was Mendelssohn's
> 42nd Psalm 'As the Hart Pants,' (which some of
> our contemporaries, comically enough printed so
> as to describe a pulsation of the human thorax.")

The Bulletin of February 10, 1858, has a further word to say:

> "As might have been anticipated from the number
> of singers, their constant practice, and the
> support of the orchestra led by Mr. Herold, the

various choral passages were admirably rendered.
The solos were perhaps as well given as could
be expected from non-professional singers. Mrs.
La Reintree sang the solo parts in the Psalm
'As the Hart Pants'...In the second part, a
number of solos, light choruses, etc., were
given. Mrs. Shattuck delivered Handel's sacred
song, 'I Know that My Redeemer Livith' in a
sweet and expressive manner....

"Towards the close of the entertainment, the
President of the Society, Mr. Turner, announced
that, with one exception in March next, no more
public concerts would probably be given by the
association...The public--which had patronized
these concerts more liberally than other series
of concerts had ever been patronized before--he
appeared to think could not appreciate the
classical music of this society, and therefore,
to make its concerts acceptable, that body had
to perform lower class pieces. This, hereafter,
it could not do, and hence it was better to stop
giving public concerts altogether. Perhaps Mr.
Turner is so far right. The public insists
upon being amused, not instructed. If the Society will give concerts for a price, they cannot expect a general audience to be content for
their dollar, with dry, tedious compositions,
which the members of the Society perform chiefly for the sake of musical practice in harmony,
and they should not court popular approbation.
The public never asked them to give open concerts. It was therefore a gratuitous piece of
impertinence on the part of Mr. Turner to talk
as he did."

The various choral societies often appeared as assisting artists with visiting celebrities. One such instance
was the farewell concert of Signora Abalos at Musical Hall,
April 3, 1856, in which the Harmonie and Germania Societies
lent their aid.

PROGRAMME

Part I

1 Overture......................Full Orchestra
2 Chorus, Sung by Members of the San Francisco
      Harmonic
3 Cavatina,from Lucia di Lammermoor......Donizetti
                Madam Abalos
4 Messenger of Spring Waltz...............Gung'l
5 Airs Finale.............from Lucrezia Borgia
                Madam Abalos

Part II

6 Overture to Iphigenia.................Mozart
7 Chorus..
8 Satanella Polka.......................Rossel
9 Spanish Canzione...................Butaguita
                Madam Abalos

         Director...........Mr. Herold

THE GERMANIA PHILHARMONIC

The German Philharmonic Society was closely allied
with the Turnverein and usually held their Sunday afternoon
concerts at the Verein Hall. In conjunction with the musical
program, stage plays were given, with dancing and singing as
added attractions. These entertainments were so popular that
even an editorial blast from the Bulletin condemning the im-
propriety of such Sabbath pleasures had little effect.

An illustration of the coordination of the several
groups is seen in the following, quoted from the Pioneer for
July, 1854, page 57:

> "'Le Désert.' Ode Symphonie by Félicien David.
> This magnificent work was produced at Musical
> Hall on Wednesday evening, June 21, to a crowd-
> ed and fashionable house, by a very full or-
> chestra, and a chorus composed of all the mem-
> bers of the Sängerbund and Philharmonic Society.

The solos were rendered by Mr. J. B. Buetler;
the recitations (sic) most admirably given by
S. W. Leach, while these two performers were
assisted in the principal parts by Messers. J.
Connor Smith and Zander. Due to the tremendous
expense and training to produce this work it
had only been produced once before in this
country. It is only doing simple justice to
say that we have never listened to a more perfect performance, and we hope that it will not
be withdrawn until every person--man, woman and
child--has heard 'Le Désert' at least once."

The year 1856 heard an especially fine series of

subscription concerts under the direction of Mr. Herold, with

Charles Kohler as leader. For these Signor and Signora Garbato

and Mrs. Julia Gould Collins were engaged as assisting ar-

tists. A novelty number was "The Firemen's March," a compo-

sition by Signor Garbato which, "Dedicated to the San Fran-

cisco Fire Department, will be produced for the first time by

a full orchestra." The Bulletin is quoted:

February 12th:

"As these concerts will be conducted with more
magnificance than any that have been given before on the Pacific Coast, they will doubtlessly meet with the approval and patronage of all
lovers of music."

March 1st:

"The second subscription concert was well attended by a larger number of ladies than any
concert previously given in this city. The performances, both vocal and instrumental, were
warmly applauded, and appeared to give every
satisfaction to the large and appreciative audience present."

PROGRAM OF THE GERMANIA SOCIETY
MUSICAL HALL
Bush Street

Fourth Subscription Concert
of the
Germania Concert Society

Friday Evening, March 28, 1856

Mrs. Julia Gould Collins will sing three of her charming pieces.

Mr. C. Koppitz, the distinguished Flutist, will play the "Carnival of Venice."

The Orchestra of the Society consists of thirty of the best Musicians in the State under the direction of Mr. Rudolph Herold.

PROGRAMME

Part I

1 Overture to Oberon............C. M. von Weber
2 Apollo Sounds, Waltz.................Labitsky
3 Robert, toi que jaime--from the Opera
    of Robert le Diable...............Meyerbeer
            Mrs. Julia Gould Collins
4 The Carnival of Venice..................Ernst
    Adapted to Flute, and executed by
            C. Koppitz
5 Adagio, Scherzo and Finale........from L. Von
    Beethoven's Grand Symphonie in C Minor

Part II

6 The Tranquility of the Ocean and a Happy
    Voyage
    Grand Descriptive Overture......Mendelssohn
    Played for the first time in California
7 Grand Scene and Cavatina from the Opera
    The Ambassadress......................Adam
            Mrs. Julia Gould Collins
8 Rubezahl Gallopp......................Ressel
9 The Merry Zingara.....................Balfe
            Mrs. Julia Gould Collins

Subscription tickets, six for $5, and single tickets at $1.50, to be had at Atwill's Music Store, Washington Street, Scheiden's Bookstore, Sacramento Street, Salvator Rosa's Music Store, Clay Street, and at the Hall on the day of the Concert.

Seats can be secured on Friday morning, from 11
to 2 o'clock, at Musical Hall.

All pieces performed at these concerts are for
sale at Atwill's Music Store.

Doors open at 7 o'clock. Concert to commence
precisely at 8 o'clock.

TO IMPROVE HEALTH

The German Turnverein organized in 1853 and elected
Charles King as president. Their meeting place was on Vallejo
Street below Stockton. "The object of this society," as the
City Directory stated, "is to maintain liberal political and
religious principles, to encourage morality, to improve
health, and to cultivate music." Soule, in the Annals of San
Francisco, pages 493 and 445 respectively, writes:

> "The Germans at this time showed a great inter-
> est in local affairs. The professional musi-
> cians in San Francisco were principally Germans,
> and in 1853 we note among a list of miscellan-
> eous facts these; the Philharmonic Society, the
> Turnvereus (sic) (Gymnastic Society) the Sänger-
> bund (Singer's Band) the San Francisco Verein,
> and the German Club.
>
> "May Day was celebrated very enthusiastically
> in 1853, the most active group being the Tur-
> ner Gesang Verein (Gymnastic Musical Union.)
> They marched 'with banners flying, and musical
> instruments sounding, to the gardens of Mr.
> Russ, near the Mission Road.' There they cele-
> brated by dancing, singing, drinking, and smok-
> ing all day. Of course, 'Das Deutsche' was
> sung ardently."

Miska Hauser, the famous violinist, tells about the
Turnverein's first May Festival most eloquently in his letter
of May 4, 1853:

> "We had a marvelous supper at the Governor's
> house after our performance was over. When we
> arrived home the German Liedertafel came to

each of our homes to serenade us while half of the population listened. All in all it could truly have been called a festive night.

"No other effort to unite the German people has been as successful as the singing societies. Their fine social affairs, often repeated and always welcome, give the true and maybe the only splendor in the social life of Germans in California. The brave German 'Saenger,' who truly deserve their good name, are to be thanked. It certainly is admirable of them to find so much time after days of hard work and struggle for self-preservation, to organize and give performances of such excellent calibre.

"With music and flying banners, the singers paraded by torch light through the streets of San Francisco, the women folk greeting them from open windows, and throwing corsages, wreaths, and other signs of approval from their windows. It was the women too who donated many of their magnificent flags.

"The celebration lasted till deep into the night. It seemed that the local brewers and singers were in cahoots--there was always something left for the singers, while all other people either had to pay ten-fold, or go thirsty. Sometimes the Yankees were chagrined, but after all it was only due to German humor and German thinking that they helped one another. No trespassing of social etiquette occurred during the whole procedure. Everything went off very properly--I almost forgot I was in San Francisco."

The Turnverein was composed of eighty members, of which thirty were in the vocal department. Besides this there existed, in connection with the Social Turnverein Association, a school for boys from seven to eighteen years, which in 1857 numbered ninety-five pupils.

The Turnverein was the father organization and center of all other German activities in the city. On special occasions, such as the May festivals, all German groups lent

their services to help make it a success. This association
of clubs was called the Turner-Gesang-Verein, and the esprit
de corps among them made their activities exceedingly successful. (For Choral Societies, see Appendix D.)

CENTER OF MAY DAY FESTIVALS

Most important event of the year for the Turnverein
was, of course, the May Day Festival celebration of their
patriotic hopes. These took on much of the activities of the
old Guild Fairs, with parades, speeches, dancing, singing,
concerts, picnics, and prizes awarded to the successful in
athletic events. In later years, after the organization of
Turnvereins in the interior towns, San Francisco was the center of the May Festivals and invited the entire membership of
clubs in neighboring towns to participate. This was made a
gala event in which out of town delegations were met at the
train by brass bands and banners, and escorted in a grand
parade to the Pacific Gardens, typical Old World German beer
garden, at the corner of Third and Harrison Streets opposite
South Park, or to the Russ Gardens, situated on the edge of
town out the Mission Road.

These festivals became an annual celebration in
1853 and usually lasted three days, with the various events
during the afternoons and evenings, after which there was
dancing until the early hours of the following day. The Wide
West of May 18, 1856, is quoted:

> "Music, dancing, oratory, gymnastics, eating and
> drinking, constituted the main features of the

festival,at which several thousand persons were
present. Notwithstanding the heterogeneous
character of the assemblage, composed as it was
of representatives of numerous nationalities of
all classes, everything passed off in an orderly and decorous manner. On the second day of
the festival, a delegation from the American
gymnasium in this city, visited the garden, and
joined in the athletic sports, acquitting themselves very accreditably.

"An unfortunate accident occurred in the premature discharge of a cannon on the second day
of the festival, by which one person was killed
and another maimed for life. It is not improper
to mention in this connection that the Association, with a liberality which is praisworthy,
especially when it is considered that the unfortunate men were not among its members, provided for the attendment, the interment of the
former, with appropriate ceremonies, and sub-
scribed $500 for the relief of the survivor."

MUSIC IN THE TURNVEREIN

The Turnverein however, musically speaking, was not
as active or successful as they were socially and gymnasti-
cally. The reason appears to be not so much a fault of their
own work as the fact that the various other German choral societies were more aggressive and overshadowed them. An ex-
planation of the following curious entry in the Wide West for
December 7, 1856, is found in the fact that the arrival of a
large steamer was so rare and important an event in those
days that news of such happening was sufficient cause to empty churches and concert halls at a moment's notice.

"In spite of the excitement in the city conse-
quent on the arrival of the steamer on Sunday
evening last, there was a good attendance at
the concert at Turnverein Hall. The performances passed off satisfactorily. Mrs. Hegelund
has a sweet voice, and when she succeeds in

overcoming her embarassment in appearing before
an audience, and is thus able to throw a little
more spirit into her efforts, she will doubtlessly become a great favorite. The orchestra
was well drilled and performed with correctness
and good effect. This evening a fine program
is presented, comprising music from 'Zampa' and
'William Tell,' as well as an operatic selection
to be rendered by Mrs. Hegelund, and other entertainments. We hope this series of Sunday
evening concerts will be kept up, but are somewhat fearful that Turnverein Hall in the rainy
season will prove so inaccessible as to defeat
the projectors of the enterprise. Would it not
be well to shift the locale of these entertainments to Musical Hall?"

GERMAN MUSICAL FESTIVALS

The highest point of musical activity by the Germans was the periodic music festival, sometimes called a Jubilee, which began in 1857. These were a grand combination
of all the numerous German music societies in the city and
state.

Daily Herald, July 24, 1857:

"The celebration of the First Annual German
Festival in California was commenced last night,
by the reception of invited guests belonging to
the different German Singing and Musical Societies in the interior. At eight o'clock the
City Societies met at the headquarters, (Turnverein Hall) and formed in order. At nine o'
clock all was in readiness, and the procession
marched to the steamboat landing. Before elev-
en o'clock the steamer arrived, and the invited
guests were received with cordial welcome...
Chief Marshall, Dr. Carl Precht, and two aides,
Messrs. Sack and Heisterberg, on horseback;
brass band, thirty instruments; California Fu-
sileer, Capt. Seidenstriker, as escort; Turnverein Society in uniform, forty eight men;
invited guests from the country, numbering about
fifty men; Eintracht Singing Society, forty-
five men; San Francisco Harmonie, fifty men...
The festival will continue four days..."

The San Francisco Bulletin, August 22, 1861:

> "Commencement of the German Musical Jubilee.
> This evening, the German Musical Jubilee will
> commence, when the San Francisco Clubs, The
> 'Harmonie' and 'Entracht' will receive the sing-
> ing clubs of the interior, on their arrival on
> board the steamer from Sacramento, and escort
> them to headquarters at Turnverein Hall......On
> Saturday, at 12 noon there will be a grand re-
> hearsal at the same place, with full orchestra,
> to which admission may be had on payment of
> $1. In the evening, a grand vocal and instru-
> mental concert, to be executed by about 200
> vocalists and 40 instrumentalists, will be
> given in the Metropolitan Theatre, under the
> direction of Mr. Herold--admission to dress
> circle and parquette, $2. Our advertising
> columns tell what next will be done, to the
> close of the Jubilee."

The San Francisco Bulletin, August 24, 1861:

> "A cantata, or 'musical picture' entitled 'A
> Night on the Sea'--music by W. Tochirich--will
> form the second part of the concert."

Much credit must be given the Germans for their lavish part in laying the foundation for San Francisco's musical heritage. Without these choral societies, participated
in by so many persons, it is doubtful whether music would
have been so well attended. These groups laid the background
and built up the audiences that were to patronize so well
the music institutions of a later day.

CHAPTER SEVEN: FIRST CONCERT ORCHESTRAS

he first concerts were heard in   saloons
of the city and the best of these were the
"Promenade Concerts" at the Arcade Saloon
in May of 1852. Music as well as   most
entertainment in early San Francisco had
its roots in the Barbary Coast. The Prom-
enade Concerts have been called the forerunner of the future
symphony because the orchestra for these affairs was the most
complete the city had yet seen.

MUSICAL MECCA

San Francisco was a mecca of musicians of all kinds
and degrees of artistry, and there seemed to be no trouble in
gathering together enough competent musicians to make up an
orchestra.   Seldom do the orchestras of that day show any
stability of membership and it appears that these groups
flowed in and out of each other, numbering either more or
less, as the exigencies of the occasion demanded.

Programs of the early '50's likewise exhibited a
want of uniformity because the restless audiences demanded
a wide variety of attractions.   Even as great an artist as
Miska Hauser soon learned this secret of success in San Francisco. An excerpt from one of Hauser's letters bearing the

date April 1, 1853, is quoted as follows:

> "It is an impossibility to give a concert in
> San Francisco without other performers. The
> more variety the better. Except for Miss Hayes
> and a Spanish lady there are at the present no
> other singers well enough liked by the public.
> All others were forced to quit. I will recruit
> a quartett and if possible a whole orchestra.
> Here are plenty of musicians, who pop up like
> mushrooms and succeed best in the hothouse atmo-
> sphere of local gambling houses and it is not
> uncommon that some lucky gambler throws a lump
> of gold from the sky to have them play 'Yankee
> Doodle' or a 'Strauss's Waltz.'"

A musical concert frequently consisted of symphonic pieces, grand opera arias, ballad quartets, a full choral society, solos for a piano, violin, or flute, and solos by tenor, basso or soprano. Many of the performers were professional musicians, but some, generally singers, were amateurs active mainly for social reasons. Reviews for such concerts often state that Mrs. Hegelund or Mrs. Shattuck, and others, were very timid before their audience and infer a studied kindliness when criticising the singer's ability. The frequent benefit concerts for artists, church, or charity, with all services contributed gratis, were particularly make-shift as far as program was concerned.

LODER: FIRST CONDUCTOR

Founder of orchestral music in San Francisco was George Loder who started in the theatres and soon organized the first Philharmonic Society. His name first occurs in connection with the American Theatre on March 22, 1852, when

he led the orchestra at the debut of the famous Madame Elisa
Biscaccianti, coloratura diva extraordinary who taught the
rude miners their first lessons in a gentle art. Mr. Loder's
debut was not as successful as the diva's, judging from comments in the <u>Alta California</u> of the following day:

> "The performance commences with a grand over-
> ture from Rossini's 'Barber of Seville.' Bar-
> ring a slight faux pas in the commencement, it
> was tolerably executed; but the orchestra is so
> weak in numbers that the whole piece seemed lit-
> tle more than a faint outline of Rossini's
> splendid creation."

A week later this same paper notes that during the
fourth concert of Mme. Biscaccianti "the orchestra performed
two overtures admirably, and they are very rapidly improving
under the direction of that excellent musician, Mr. Loder."
In the successive concerts of this series he was praised for
his flute obligato to a coloratura aria for Biscaccianti and
for his new song "Greeting to California," poem by Alfred
Wheeler, the first song ever dedicated to a San Francisco woman.

On June 17, Loder directed the orchestra for the
benefit tendered Miska Hauser, the celebrated Hungarian violinist, who had just completed his concert series and later
in that year he was musical director for the operatic costume
concerts of Catherine Hayes. These were given with only the
assistance of a baritone and soprano, Herr Mengis and Miss
Coad, and there was no chorus, no scenery of any magnitude,
and no orchestra of operatic size.

From these crude beginnings there arose the San
Francisco Philharmonic Society which was to make itself the
leading music organization of the city for several years to
come. The earliest mention of this group occurs in an advertisement of October 24, 1852:

> "Mr. George Loder, musical director of the San
> Francisco Philharmonic Society, respectfully
> informs his friends and the public, that, hav-
> ing finished his tour through the interior he
> has permanently the exercise of his profession
> in all its branches, Viz:
>
> "Lessons given in singing, upon the pianoforte,
> organ and flute, pianoforte tuning and the se-
> lections of instruments, etc.
>
> "From his long experience and practical know-
> ledge of the manufacture of pianofortes, etc.
> he begs to offer his services to those parties
> who may wish to purchase instruments, knowing
> that the inspection and guarantee of the excel-
> lence of the workmanship will enhance the value
> of the purchase."

An early triumph was his direction of the Philharmonic for the concert series of the Pacific Musical Troupe at
the newly built Musical Hall, beginning in July of 1853 and
extending well into the following year. At this time his orchestra was "strong and well selected, consisting of sixteen
instruments." A few of the purely orchestral offerings during this series of fourteen concerts included the overtures
"Le Roi D'Yvetot," "La Dame Blanche," and "Fra Diavolo," as
well as the accompaniment for many choral and operatic pieces,
ballads and such great works as Haydn's "Creation," "The
Seasons," and Felicien David's "The Desert."

A public tribute was given Mr. Loder by Ole Bull,
the great violin virtuoso, for his services in conducting the

orchestral accompaniment of that master. The occasion was
Ole Bull's farewell concert at the Metropolitan Theatre July
28, 1854, and the Daily Herald reports it thus:

> "At the close of this masterpiece, 'The Carni-
> val of Venice,' the great violinist was called
> out and saluted as usual with tumultuous ap-
> plause. Selecting one of the bouquets that fell
> around him, he advanced to the footlights and
> gracefully presented it to Mr. Loder, leader of
> the orchestra--a recognition of that gentleman's
> merits that met with a ready and hearty applause
> from the audience."

After the completion of this series of concerts,
little else was heard of Mr. Loder and his Philharmonic Society until a newspaper notice of July 8, 1855, which stated
that he was conducting promenade concerts for fifty-cent ad-
missions, at the Russ Gardens, scene of the early Turnverein
May Festivals. In 1856 he left for Australia, where he died
the following year. Thereafter honors as the leading orchestra in the city went to the Germania Philharmonic Society under the leadership of Mr. Rudolph H. Herold.

HEROLD: FIRST CHORAL DIRECTOR

The destiny and art of the Germania Philharmonic
Society, as well as that of numerous choral groups of
which he was director, were bound up in the personality of Mr.
Rudolph H. Herold, who has often been called the founder of
San Francisco's musical heritage. Mr. Herold arrived here
November 20, 1852, as the piano accompanist of Catherine
Hayes, and remained to become the city's first man of music.

He was not the first to achieve fame as an orchestral leader, as we have seen, but he was undoubtedly the greatest.

The activities of Mr. Herold were almost inseparable from the Turnverein and the several German choral societies of the city. Orchestral concerts, choral society concerts, benefit concerts, the German May Festivals, the many special vocal concerts and, more often than not, a combination of these follow throughout the '50's and '60's in a bewildering maze, but throughout all there was the leadership of Mr. Herold.

THE GERMANIA PHILHARMONIC SOCIETY

The origin and background of the Germania is very well told in a brochure entitled June Music Festival, June, 1883, in the possession of the De Young Museum Library:

> "Our people are not entirely elementary in their taste and knowledge, though our advantages have been less than those of cities nearer the Atlantic seaboard. Our musical beginnings were small. In 1853 there was no instrumental music independent of the theatres which employed not more than seven in the orchestra. The gambling-houses which added music to their numerous blandishments, employed about the same number. In 1853 a string band calling itself the 'Verandah Concert Society' was organized. Its list of members included the familiar names of Charles Kohler, Charles Koppitz, John Frohling, Charles Schutz, Boehm, Buchel, and a few others, all of them excellent instrumentalists. Out of this band grew the Germania Society, a musical organization that endured for many years, and which introduced itself to the public by a series of Sunday Evening Concerts given with an orchestra of twenty-eight pieces at the Turnverein Hall on Bush Street, then just erected.

The place became popular at once, and though it
was small, and the admission price only fifty
cents,the receipts were sometimes eighteen hundred dollars in a single evening. Among the
noted musicians who appeared here in connection
with the orchestra were Madame Anna Bishop,
Bochsa, the harpist, Lanzoni, a celebrated baritone of that time, and Buetler, a tenor of
repute..."

Two series of concerts by the Germania Philharmonic

occurred in 1855, beginning in January and May respectively.

The Daily Herald report of May 21st, indicates that this so-

ciety was yet in its pioneering stage:

"This admirable resort for refined amusement was
well filled last evening, by an audience drawn
thither to listen to the harmonies of the second concert of the new series. As usual, the
music was excellent, and excited the warmest
applause throughout the evening. Two capital
overtures were given--Boieldieu's 'La Dame
Blanche' and Weber's celebrated 'Jubilee Overture,' composed in honor of the birthday of the
King of Saxony. This last, on account of its
classical nature, and the numerous difficult
passages that abound in it, has many require-
ments which the Germanians, on account of the
smallness of their numerical force, necessarily
fail to come up to. In fact, we doubt if it
could be given as it should be, in order to af-
ford entire satisfaction, and numbering at
least fifty or sixty performers. As it is, however, the Germanians made the most of it that
could have been done under the circumstances.
Mr. Simonson executed De Beriot's 'Fifth Air'
in very excellent taste, and very free from the
ordinary ranting and wildness which at times
disfigures this gentleman's playing. A very
fine duo for the cornet and trombone,by Messers.
Yak and Buchel, was performed; but we think the
finest of the selections for the evening, consisted in the rendition of an aria and chorus
from 'Lucrezia' by the brass instruments. This
was certainly admirable, and in reply to an encore, they gave one of Gung'l's Gallopes, with
a precision and celerity of movement that was
worthy of exceeding praise. The usual quantity
of quadrille and waltz music by Strauss and
other composers, was interspersed throughout
the entertainment."

At a later concert of this second series Rossini's overture, "The Siege of Corinth," was given in a masterful manner and "Der Freischütz" drew down a hurricane of applause.

A description of the Germania Philharmonic is found in the following quotation from the San Francisco Daily Herald of October 26, 1855:

"Those who were fortunate enough to be present at the masterly entertainment given last evening for the benefit of Mr. Herold, the accomplished leader of the Germanians, were the recipients of a most delightful treat. The orchestra on this occasion embraced the flower of the profession, and was, without exception, the best graduated and evenly constructed force we have had the pleasure of listening to in California. To a force of thirteen stringed instruments, consisting of four first and five second violins, two double basses and two violoncelli, there were added twelve brass and reed instruments, viz: two grand clarionettes, two bassoons, one hautboy, two French horns, two cornets and one trombone. Kettle and bass drums, triangle, etc. made up the band, which, formed of twenty-six instruments, were in capital drill and went through their at once arduous and classic duties with a correctness and vigor in the highest degree complimentary to the skill and training of their accomplished 'Chef.' The opening overture was selected from Weber, and his ever glorious 'Oberon,' filled with lightly tripping measures so suggestive of fairies, and of all the mazy magic weaving that Shakespeare has thrown around the theme, was placed before the force for rendition. This was done in excellent style and time, and but few, very few of the heavier and more labored passages occurring in the 'score' were slurred in the execution. As a whole, for the number of instruments employed, we have rarely or never heard it more perfectly given, even in lands more favored numerically speaking, and, too, where none of the drawbacks which are necessarily the rule here are experienced. Following the overture Gung'l's truly delightful waltz of 'Wanderlieder' was given by the instrumental force, and abounding as the composition does in those excessive dashes of waving and salutary melody under the

full rendition of the orchestra, it seemed to
gather new beauties and become more intensely
brilliant in their hands. A pleasing little melody by Kuecken, sung simply and pleasingly by
Miss Van den Broeck, and Fuerstenau's intricate
and brilliant flute solo 'L'Illusion,' performed
in his usual happy and effective manner, by Mr.
C. Koppitz, and Mendelssohn's majestic and thrill-
ing 'Wedding March' from his unfinished opera of
'A Midsummer Night's Dream' was given by the orchestra."

In the succeeding year there were again two series
of concerts, one in March and April which featured Signora
Abalos and Mrs. Julia Gould Collins as soloists, and one in
December, marked by the appearance of Mrs. Amanda Hegelund,
who both sang and played piano numbers. The overtures "William Tell" and "Zampa" were featured by the orchestra.

In the February series of the third year the Germania was again successful. One program included the "Concert
Overture in D Minor " by "Kalliwoda," Flotow 's overture to
"Martha," and the first movement of Mozart's "Grand Sinfonia
in C Major" as well as songs of Max Zorer, a serenade on the
French horn by Mr. A. Lapfgeer and dance music by Strauss
and Lanner. The November concerts were a failure, however,
the reason for which is explained in Wide West of November
15, 1857:

"The last of these entertainments were given
last evening by the Germania Society. We regret
to learn that the season has not proved a
profitable one for the projectors of the entertainments. This result might have been antici-
pated at the outset. To fill such a hall as
the Pavillion, from a small community, three
times a week, was an undertaking that could only
be accomplished by establishing a very low rate
for prices of admission. Such a course would

have secured the presence of a sufficient crowd
to keep the Pavillion warm by very force of
numbers, and would thus have done away with the
complaints of chilliness so prevalent during
the latter part of the series of concerts; a
condition not at all alleviated by the staring
'Ice Cream' placards prominently displayed. The
musical portion of the entertainments has been
excellent, tho' perhaps it would have been more
pleasing had it comprised more 'familiar' music.
The first time of hearing a piece seldom en-
ables one to fully appreciate its merit...Nov-
elty, however, is so uncommon an accompaniment
of San Francisco performances, that we are in
no humor to find fault on this ground. We trust
ere long to learn that the Germania concerts
have been resumed under more favorable aus-
pices."

The Germania, however, did not give any more concerts until February of 1860, and during this interval there
were few formal concerts of orchestral music. Even this latter series was not particularly successful, for when the concerts were again resumed in October under very different
circumstances, a new conductor lifted his baton to lead them.
The following program was heard at Platt's New Music Hall:

"Grand Vocal and Instrumental concert will be
given on Saturday evening, October 6, 1860 by
Ryster's Italian and English Opera Company in
conjunction with the Germania Philharmonic Society numbering over thirty performers."

Conductor: A. Reiff, Jr.

PROGRAMME

Part I

1 Overture, Der Freischütz................Weber
          Philharmonic Society
2 Song......................Mr. Stephen Leach
3 Potpourri, The Jolly Figaro...........Streck
          Philharmonic Society
4 Aria, Ave Maria....................Schubert
          Miss Rosalie Durand

5 Old English Ballad,
    Sally in our Alley...................Carey
6 Waltz, Lebensbilder Lebensbelden.....Labitzky
    Philharmonic Society

Part II

1 Overture, Maritana....................Wallace
    Philharmonic Society
2 Cavatina, Favorite...................Donizetti
    Mme. Lucy Escott
3 Song, Maniac.........................Russell
    Mr. J. De Haga
4 Romance, Sweet Mountain Home............Tully
    Miss Georgia Hodson
5 Aria, La Donnac' Mobile (Rigoletto)......Verdi
    Mr. Henry Squires
6 Laughing Trio
        Opera Company
7 Grand March
        Philharmonic Society

FIDDLERS FOR THESPIS

Every theatre in the city had its own orchestra
composed of professional musicians, whose duties included
playing the customary overtures between acts, accompanying
singers in the specialty songs interspersed throughout the
drama (a peculiar custom in vogue at the time) and of being
prepared to play the orchestral scores of operas when an operatic troupe was booked at the theatre.

One of the best known of the theatre orchestra leaders was Signor Bochsa, who came to San Francisco with the
company of Madame Anna Bishop, the operatic diva, on February
2, 1854. For the next two years his name appears on many
concert, benefit, and theatre programs. Sometimes he played
the harp; sometimes the piano. On one occasion he led the Germania Philharmonic and for two years he was director of the

Metropolitan Theatre, located on Montgomery Street between Washington and Jackson. "Norma" and "La Sonnambula" were two of the favorite operas given by Madame Bishop which he led from the orchestra pit. (See Chapter 11.)

Other musicians in the theatres were Mr. Chas. Koppitz, who led the orchestra at Maguire's Opera House on its re-opening, June 7, 1858; Herr Kohler, director of the Union Band, at the opening performance of the first German Theatre, Armory Hall, May 15, 1853; George H. Williams, director for the Backus Minstrels; Mr. Smith, director at the Jenny Lind Theatre, who took a benefit January 26, 1863; and, during 1864, the New Idea Theatre had for music directors George H. Edmonds, L. Mundwiller, and Harry Williams. An unfortunate occurrence was the death of Mr. Napier Lothian, member of the American Theatre orchestra, who died December 12, 1854, with his baton in his hand, after conducting for a ball given by the San Francisco Blues.

Briefly mentioned as leaders of orchestras are Signor Bona, grand promenade concert and ball at Musical Hall, 1854; C. A. Andres, Turnverein May Festival at Russ Gardens, in 1867; Mr. Louis Schmidt, concert of Martin and Fanny Simonson at Platt's New Music Hall, 1863; Mr. G. A. Scott, grand promenade concert at Musical Hall, 1858; Signor Bona, benefit to Mme. Biscaccianti, American Theatre, April 29, 1852; and Charles Kohler, leader of Amateur Musical Club, Musical Hall, October 3, 1856; Mr. Plaud, leader of orchestra at Adelphi Theatre concert on July 1, 1855.

Two items of peculiar interest appear in the <u>Alta California</u> of October 17, 1852 and January 14, 1853 respectively:

> "The celebrated Chinese Dramatical Company, known as the Tong Hook Co., will give tomorrow evening at the American Theatre a performance of their own. It consists of 123 performers accompanied by an orchestra of their own music, and under the management of Messers. Tiksoon, Norman Assing, and Tong Chick. They appear in a beautiful spectacle, 'The Eighth Genii.'"

> "Amongst the itinerant bands of minstrels in this town, is one which consists of an Italian drummer, with triangle accompaniment, and a reed instrument fastened to his mouth. A hand organist with triangle, and boy collector with the same instrument complete the orchestra accompaniment. The music is really good, and the foreign 'Musicianers' pick up 'quarters' very lively."

CHAMBER MUSIC

Chamber music, as we know it today, is of somewhat recent origin. Nowhere in the early history of music in San Francisco has there been found a specific allusion to chamber music. A number of musical programs by small orchestras do occur however, and by loosely applying the term we may be justified in calling them chamber music organizations. The earliest of these was founded by the violin virtuoso, Miska Hauser, and was originated for identically the same purpose that chamber music first came into being: to provide music by a limited orchestra in a small chamber and produced mainly for the personal gratification of the performers; earlier, composers, such as Bach, Haydn, Mozart, and Beethoven were often employed to write for the pleasure of aristocratic patrons.

Miska Hauser in his collected letters, tells his own story to considerable length thus:

"I have founded a new 'Musikverein' here and have been elected its Artistic Director. We had our first rehearsal; it was an attempt, but nothing to brag about. Yet my troubles have been rewarded. Mr. Davidson, the Director of the local branch 'Haus Rothschild,' who lives in a marvelous house, is the head of the newly formed 'Musikverein' and he dedicated to me, in the name of the Verein, a 'Gededkmunze' of solid gold, easily worth more than $100. The lyre is engraved, and the insignia around it reads: 'Dem unvergesslichen violin kunstler Miska Hauser von den musik Freunden Californians!

"The Quartett which I organized so laboriously gave me for a long time more pleasure than all the gold in California. The Quartett in its perfection as Beethoven saw it, this mental Quadrologue of equally atuned souls, in itself a world of actions, passions and hope, is my savior whenever other demons with their promising offers try to bring me to the flower-clad abyss. Too bad--my viola player died of indigestion--and for some time I will miss the purest of all musical pleasures. Among the local artists is a pupil from the Vienna conservatory, who, in cooperation with other musicians, earns daily 40 to 50 dollars. All the members of my orchestra have given a very recommendable example--they do not expect pay except one contra bass player, a Bohemian.

"Lately I have been fortunate again to arrange a Quartett. Too bad that the other three were not solely satisfied with the harmonies of the Beethoven Quartet. They want a more harmonic attribute of $15 each for two hours. The sound of gold is still the most effective music.

"I am proud to have assembled an orchestra which should do honor to an European residence. I collected my musicians from the gambling houses, hired them, rehearsed them--I have given 26 concerts up to now--and finally got them to the point when I could dare to perform Beethoven's magnificent 'Lenore' overture. This concert took a full four hours, because I

had to give in to those present, Chinese and
adventurers from every country, and play three
encores (sic) to each number. And when played
a composition, using as theme a Chinese melody,
then suddenly the children of heaven expressed
their emotions with unhuman articulations and
noises, so much that I finally had to hide in
some far away corner of the theatre in order to
survive the Chinese triumph."

The several other attempts at chamber music in early
San Francisco were not as well received as Hauser's. The one
exception, however, was the Verandah Concert Society already
mentioned which called itself a "string band" and eventually
grew into the Germania Philharmonic Society. One of these
was the "New Era Concerts" of Madam Abalos and Professor
Sarles in 1856, at Musical Hall. "They were to be assisted
by a quartet orchestra under the direction of Herr Sneider."
The San Francisco Bulletin reports their failure thus:

"The concert given last night at Musical Hall
by Mme. Abalos and Prof. Sarles was very re-
spectfually attended by an audience full of
curiosity to witness the first of the 'New Era
Concerts.' Mme. Abalos and Prof. Sarles are
very clever artists in their own particular
line; but in all sincerity, we do not think
these 'New Era Concerts' will ever be appreciated by a San Francisco audience. Our community is decidedly a music-loving people, but
they require the best talent that can be had
for their money."

A concert was given at the Unitarian Church for the
purpose of purchasing a new organ, and Rossini's "Stabat Mater"
was given. In conjunction with the full orchestra was a trio
for grand piano, violoncello and violin, under Jacques Blumenthal. The program, given by an orchestra and chorus numbering about sixty "was finely done -- except an unhappy trio

for the pianoforte, violin and violoncello, which wearied the
tired audience by its grievous length."

BRASS BANDS

Band music was generally reserved for parades and
outdoor entertainments such as picnics, May Festivals, and
patriotic celebrations. A full score of brass bands are
found to have been active during the '50's and early '60's,
many of which were in connection with the Turnverein and other
German groups who were particularly fond of this type of music. (For Bands, see Appendix E.) Two celebrations of the
Turnverein are described in the San Francisco Daily Herald of
December 24, 1854 and May 6, 1855, respectively:

> "Last evening, the Turnverein Society's Hall
> was dedicated to its uses in the presence of a
> large audience, comprising about two thousand
> persons, among whom were a large number of ladies.

> "The 'Turn Hall' is a brick built edifice and
> is of oblong form, being 130 feet long by 70
> feet wide, thus presenting very fair propor-
> tions...

> "At a few minutes after eight o'clock the com-
> mittee and members of the Society who had walked
> in a procession arrived at the Hall, which was
> speedily filled by the audience, the Union Brass
> Band playing Washington's March.

> "The Band then played 'Brueden reicht dieich
> und sum bund' (Brothers, join your hands for our
> band.) This air had reference to, and was very
> popular during the German struggle in the times
> of '48."

POT POURRIS FROM MARTHA

"About $8\frac{1}{2}$ o'clock last evening the stirring
notes of a powerful band of music were heard on
our streets, and the Society of the Turnverein,

headed by the Union Cornet Band, passed along Montgomery Street, on their way to escort the up-river deputations to the 'May Feast' to their quarters. The Club turned out a goodly array of members, all neatly dressed in white linen uniforms. They carried a large number of colored lanterns, which, with the American and German colors and some transparencies, gave the whole turn-out a very gay appearance. After receiving their guests at the Vallejo street wharf, they again passed through the city, the band discoursing some pot pourris from 'Martha' and other operas in a very artistic and pleasing manner. The band was instructed to stop playing while passing houses of worship."

An advertisement in the San Francisco Bulletin of April 4, 1856 will prove interesting:

"The members of the German Brass Band gave notice that they are fully prepared to execute any kind of music wanted. They have fixed their price at $10 per hour and $50 per night or day. Director Ferdinand Pape."

Following are several items concerning brass bands and the occasions on which they performed:

San Francisco Bulletin, May 2, 1859:

German May Festival, Turnverein (People's Garden.)

"Procession, with the German Band, consisting of twenty celebrated musicians, under the direction of the well-known leader, Buechel, from the New Turner Hall, corner of California and Kearny Streets."

San Francisco Bulletin, September 8, 1857. Admission Day Parade.

"The San Francisco Brass Band, 6 men mounted. American Brass Band, leader--A. Wolcott, in gray uniform with bearskin caps. 16 men."

San Francisco Bulletin, February 19, 1858:

"The Independent National Guard, Capt. Moore, will parade on the afternoon of Monday February 22, Washington's Birthday. The American Brass Band will accompany them."

"THE BUNKER HILL ASSOCIATION
will give a
Grand Social Party
in honor of
Washington's Birthday,
at
Platt's Hall
February 20, 1863

The Band of the Ninth Regiment will be present, by the kind permission of General Wright.

J. W. Fuller's Quadrille Band of 14 pieces has also been engaged for this occasion..."

CHAPTER EIGHT: <u>MUSIC DEALERS AND INSTRUMENT MAKERS</u>

an Francisco's population growing from about one thousand people in 1848 to over twenty thousand by the end of 1849 caused a scarcity of certain commodities.   Compared with the demand for them,   musical instruments were exceedingly few.   The long arduous journey which required crossing the Isthmus   of Panama on mule-back prohibited people from bringing such   articles with them.

When the miners   established their camps, they discovered that they wanted music "to while away tedious hours" and a strong desire for accordions, violins   and   guitars, flutes and horns became prevalent.   The most humble instruments   were   treasured and   on one   occasion Stephen Massett traded a jew's harp to a Mexican boy for a lump of gold worth eight dollars, although the article had   originally been purchased at a dollar a gross.

Musical   instruments   were wanted   in the   city for dance halls, gambling houses,   and   such amusement   places as were patronized by returning lucky miners who were free with their gold when gratifying their passion for singing and dancing. To supply the demand, several pioneers became music dealers, and many of the early merchants added musical goods to their stock-in-trade. Most of them found this profitable and many remained in business after gold rush days to become rich and famous with the growing city.

FIRST MUSIC STORE OPENS

One of the first to visualize the new gold frontier as a lucrative field for merchandising of musical instruments was Andrew Kohler. When he departed for the new El Dorado in 1849, he had the foresight to bring with him a miscellaneous collection of instruments. Thus in January of 1850, in a rude structure near the foot of Broadway the A. KOHLER--MUSIC STORE, the first enterprise of its kind, opened for business. At first trade in the little shop was not confined to the sale of musical instruments; with Germanic sagacity Mr. Kohler reasoned that people must eat and shrewdly added a stock of groceries.

The store was destroyed by fire in 1851 and was rebuilt on the same site. Kohler's faith in his musical venture was justified -- it prospered -- outgrew its first humble quarters and in 1852 was removed to 272 Stockton Street. The grocery line was discontinued and a stock of 'Fancy Goods, Imported and American Toys, and Children's Clothing' were added to the line of musical instruments. The new store became known as "Santa Claus Headquarters."

By 1857 Quincy A. Chase, a nephew, had entered the business as a clerk and became of great assistance to Mr. Kohler. Trade, now largely wholesale, had increased enough to warrant the opening of a second store located at 175 Washington Street. The following advertisement which appeared in Langley's City Directory in 1858 indicates the growth and scope of the enterprise:

> "A. Kohler's Stock of Musical instruments probably exceeds the sum total of all other similar stocks in California--consequently he must and will sell CHEAP.
>
> The goods must be SOLD to make room for that IMMENSE STOCK which is now on the way from France and Germany.
>
> PIANO FORTES from different manufacturers, and warranted perfect in every particular.
>
> BRASS INSTRUMENTS--French, German, and Italian at prices varying from 75¢ to $50 each, with and without bows and cases.
>
> GUITARS--with paper or wooden cases, if required, prices greatly reduced."

Further expansion became necessary. On October 18, 1859, warerooms, described by the Mercantile Guide as "the largest music salesrooms in the state," were opened at 424 Sansome Street. On October 19, 1859 the San Francisco Call published the following:

"KOHLER'S NEW STORES"

> "A. Kohler opened his new rooms in the second story of Howard's Building on Sansome Street extending from Clay to Commercial Streets last evening. He occupies the entire floor, 120 x 65 feet--the south half as a music store and

the northern half as a wholesale store for toys
and fancy goods. A large company was present
last evening and there was music and dancing
till a late hour. In addition to these magnificent rooms, Kohler continues his stores on
Washington and Commercial Streets."

In 1860, this pioneer merchant ceased to advertise
"Piano Fortes from different manufacturers," but acquired a
very select stock of quality merchandise and was featuring
such fine instruments as: COLLARD & COLLARD PIANOS from London, PLEYEL PIANOS from Paris, MASON & HAMLIN MELODEONS and
ORGAN HARMONIUMS -- for churches and halls -- from Paris, and
BRASS & WOOD INSTRUMENTS "from all the best makers in the
world."

The exact date when music publishing was included
in the business is not known; probably in 1857, for the music department of the San Francisco Public Library has a song
inscribed as follows: Song: Here Shall We Meet by Clement
White: sung by Mr. Henry: entered according to an Act of Congress, 1857, by A. Kohler, 178 Washington Street and 276
Stockton Street.

In 1863 Kohler went to Europe on a buying trip, established an agency in Rome to facilitate purchase of the famous "Roman Strings" sought by all the "fastidious" stringed
instrument players of the time, and an agency in Germany for
a continual supply of toys. Carefully selected merchandise
and business acumen were important factors in the tremendous
growth that followed, and from these humble beginnings a
great institution developed. The firm now called Kohler and

Chase, is known internationally and is held in high   regard
by musicians and music lovers the world over.

ATWILL & COMPANY

Joseph Atwill, who had engaged in the music trade
in New York for some years, arrived in California in 1849 and
after a brief experience as a gold miner opened the second
music store in San Francisco. It was located in the Old Zinc
Building at the corner of Clay Street and Brenham Place and,
was started in September of 1850. Fortunately, the Atwill Company escaped both the disastrous fires of 1851, but needing
larger quarters was moved to 172 Washington Street in the latter part of that year. Besides being a pioneer merchant Mr.
Atwill was active in civic affairs, President of the Board of
Assistant Aldermen, and a member of the first Board of Educa-
tion. In 1854 a branch was opened in Sacramento and early
advertisements mention a branch at 201 Broadway in New York.
In addition to music and instruments the store carried a wide
assortment of goods as described in the following advertisement which appeared in Parker's Directory of 1852:

"ATWILL & CO.--MUSIC AND FANCY GOODS STORE."
172 Washington near Montgomery.
also Broadway, New York.

At this establishment the purchaser can at all
times be supplied (Wholesale and Retail) with
every description of MUSICAL INSTRUMENTS and
MUSICAL MERCHANDISE. Also TOYS, GAMES, FANCY
GOODS, PERFUMERY,STATIONERY,PRINTS, PAINTINGS,
ETC. Seminaries, Military Bands and Professors
supplied on reasonable terms.   New Music and
New Goods received by every steamer from New
York. Atwill & Co." 1

---

1 For list of music published in the Fifties, see appendix J.

Mr. Atwill had training and experience as a printer and engraver in his youth and he was undoubtedly the first to enter the music publishing business here.

An advertisement appearing in the <u>Wide West</u> on February 18, 1855 states that Dan H. Douglas became successor to Atwill; however the name of Atwill and Co. was continued and Atwill apparently remained active in the business until 1860 when he went to Virginia City in Nevada to become active in merchandising and politics.

WOODWORTH & CO.

In 1852 Woodworth & Co., a partnership between Frederick A. Woodworth, and his brother Selin E. Woodworth commenced dealing in pianos and melodeons in a store located at 130 Clay Street. They moved to 16 Montgomery Street in 1856 and became "exclusive agents in California for Stoddart Piano Fortes and Prince's Melodeons. In 1861 they moved to 28 Montgomery Street, and a year later Alfred F. Allovan joined the firm which became known as Woodworth -- Allovan & Co., moving to a new location in the Masonic Temple at 12 Post Street. Here the scope of their business was enlarged to include the importation and sale of "Church and Parlor Harmoniums, Reed and Pipe Organs."

SALVATOR ROSA

Salvator Rosa, a colorful pioneer, "who spoke little English, but knew every note and word of his native Italian opera," opened a music store at 180 Clay Street in 1852.

He dealt exclusively in musical goods and became friendly with many of the visiting celebrities who enjoyed visiting his shop. Mr. Rosa was given the "Special Premium Award" for his display of instruments at the Mechanics' Fair in 1857. He was the publisher of a ballad "Bright Things Can Never Die," by Edward F. Rimbault, which was sung with great success by Signora Bianchi at the Metropolitan Theatre. This song has remained popular through the years and is occasionally sung by present day radio artists. He was located at 193 Clay Street in 1856, 157 Montgomery Street in 1858, and 615 Montgomery Street in 1861.

MATHIAS GRAY

William Herwig, a clarinet player and music teacher, and Mathias Gray entered the music business in 1859 at 176 Clay Street. Herwig withdrew shortly and the firm was continued as M. Gray Co. Mr. Gray prospered, moved to 163 Clay Street in 1860, 613 Clay Street in 1861, and had the agency for Steinway pianos. His store was headquarters for many visiting musicians.

BADGER & LINDENBERGER

In 1857 William G. Badger, owner of a clothing and general merchandise establishment at 105 Battery Street, formed a partnership with Thomas E. Lindenberger, his former bookkeeper. They sold musical instruments and upon acquiring "the sole agency for Chickering Pianos" moved to 413 Battery Street.

RASCHE & PFLEUGER

Frederick Rasche and Herman Pfleuger opened a store at 190 Washington Street in 1856. They sold jewelry as well as music and instruments for about a year, whereupon Mr. Pfleuger withdrew; the firm became known as Rasche & Sons, and dealt exclusively in music and music publishing. They engaged in this type of business at 650 Washington Street in 1861 and moved to 131 Montgomery Street in 1862.

INSTRUMENT MAKERS OF FIFTIES

J. H. Falkenberg started the first piano factory in San Francisco in 1849 on Jackson Street. Pianos at this early date were extremely scarce, yet Mr. Falkenberg amusingly advertised that he would "tune any make piano."

ZECH: FIRST GREAT PIANO MAKER

While it was considered less expensive to import pianos than to make them here, there were several highly skilled artisans engaged in manufacturing. Of these Jacob Zech was undoubtedly the outstanding local piano maker of his time. He began making pianos at 111 Clay Street about 1855, and first came to the public attention at the Mechanics' Institute Fair in 1857, where his great talent earned public recognition and award.

The report of the Mechanics' Institute Fair, September 7, 1857 describes Jacob Zech's workmanship as follows:

"(Exhibit) 2 piano fortes--1st the best of all exhibited--square piano--$7\frac{1}{4}$ octaves in rosewood case and in tone, touch, beauty of finish

and apparent durability, is eminently superior.
Wood for the case and hardware used were imported. The metal and cedar employed in the
interior are of native growth, very hard, well
adapted to the purpose; and all the work was
done in S. F. Second in all respects similar to
the first but is slightly inferior to it in
tone. Diploma. (Highest award.)"

Frederick Zech was also a piano maker and, though
apparently less talented than his brother Jacob, was an exhibitor at a later Mechanics' Institute Fair. Frederick
Zech's factory was located at 2 Summer Street and he special-
ized in tuning and repairing pianos.

Another exhibitor was John Bender, skilled piano
maker, who lived at 3 Post Street, between Powell and Mason.

Margaret Blake Alverson mentions other instrument
craftsmen of the fifties. In her book Sixty Years of California Song, she states:

"A celebrated artist in his line was Urban, the
violin repairer. Phaff the flute and clarinet
man was another. 1 Others were Senor Mojica,
maker of guitars; harps in Italian quarter of
Kearny Street; Charles Morrill, of banjos; Tall
Dan Delaney, drummer at Maguire's Theatre (who
wouldn't learn a note of music and played as he
pleased) who repaired drums and C. C. Keene,
maker of accordions, in former days much played."

Joseph Urban made and repaired guitars, violins and
other stringed instruments. His exhibit at the Mechanics'
Fair in 1857 was reported as follows:

"Joseph Urban, San Francisco--a guitar and two
violins. Guitar was the only one exhibited.
Superior in both tone and finish. It has the

---

1 An example of variation in name spelling of the fifties:
Langley's City Directory gives Plaff, Alverson says Phaff;
others, Paffs, Pfaff.

peculiarity of three additional strings which
may be tuned as a bass accompaniment to any key
at the will of the performer. One of the violins is an alto and both are excellent. They
give evidence of decided talent, and will not
suffer by comparison, either of style or tone
with the best imported. Diploma."

Mr. George Plaff was another exceptionally skilled
artisan who came a little later. He first advertised in
Langley's City Directory in 1860 and was a manufacturer of
flutes and clarinets. Report of the committee of the fifth
Mechanics' Fair held in 1865 describe his work as follows:

"Flutes of George Plaff, San Francisco, who exhibited a case containing a variety of flutes
of his own manufacture. These flutes were superior in tone and workmanship to any exhibited
before. In addition to the usual keys and o-
penings in imported flutes, Mr. Plaff has added
several others, which improves them to a considerable extent, as they enable the player to execute with greater ease than heretofore very
difficult passages, keys and shakes. The instruments of Mr. Plaff are bored in a more perfect manner, which also improves the sound.
Awarded a diploma."

Other pioneer instrument makers whose workmanship drew favorable comment at early Mechanics' Fairs were:

Mr. C. C. Keene, who manufactured flutinas and accordions at 103 Montgomery Street; and Charles Stumcke who
was awarded "a bronze medal for a handsome harp-guitar at the
exhibition of 1857."

ORGAN BUILDERS

Organ building was introduced here by Robert Farran
and John McCraith who began this type of work in 1859. Others

who advertised as "organ builders" were: B. Shellard, Montgomery, near Green Street, 1859; Joseph Mayer, 725 Montgomery
Street, 1861; Woodworth, Allovan & Co., 12 Post Street, 1862,
and W. S. Pierce, 26 Montgomery Street, 1863.

Organs of a number of the principal churches were
constructed here, and in later years several excellent instruments of high cost were built for churches throughout the
state.

During the fifties it appeared that San Francisco
might become a center of instrument manufacturing. The early
demand for instruments, particularly pianos, increased and
the importation and sale of instruments remained profitable
for years. Just what prevented greater development of the
industry here is hard to say; but a score of years after the
first factory was started by Falkenberg "there were about one
hundred and twenty pianos made annually in the city." This
was little compared with production of mammoth factories
which by this time were established in Boston, New York,
Baltimore and Philadelphia. Statistics show that during 1869
about twenty-five thousand pianos at a value of seven million
dollars were produced in the United States.

CHAPTER NINE: MINSTRELS AND MINSTRELSY

 edieval France had its jongleurs, Germany
its minnesingers, Scotland   its   border
minstrels, Wales its bards;   and the harp
of Ireland sounded not only "through Ta-
ra's Halls" but many other places.   There
were minstrels of a vagabond   nature   a-
mong the vaqueros of Spanish California, the wandering   serenaders who journeyed about the country from pueblo to rancho
and to mission singing and playing for their hosts and bene-
factors.   The roving troubadors passed from the scene and were
supplanted in California in 1849 by a new type of minstrel.

THE BEGINNINGS OF MINSTRELSY

Like their predecessors of olden times, blackface
minstrels were usually gripped with wanderlust and it is not
surprising that they were among the first to answer the cry
of 'Gold in California!' The Philadelphia Minstrels began an
engagement at the Bella Union on October 22, 1849. The New
York Minstrels arrived about the same time and appeared at
Washington Hall. Both were well received and on October 25,
1849 the Pacific News recommended the Philadelphia Minstrels
as follows:

"Our citizens have been favored during the week
by the truly amusing concerts of the above band.

> They are eight in numbers and their instruments
> are well selected. Three times a week they
> give concerts at the Bella Union Hall, entrance
> on Washington Street; we would advise all lov-
> ers of fun to go and hear them."

On October 27, 1849, the same paper stated:

> "The New York Minstrels made their second ap-
> pearance at Washington Hall in this city on
> Thursday evening. We learn that the entertain-
> ments of the evening were truly Ethiopian in
> character and that Messrs. Crow, Jumbow and Co.
> were greeted with great applause. May their
> efforts to please fill their pockets with yel-
> low stuff."

The term Negro Minstrel is a misnomer; real negroes
did not enter this profession until 1862. It was so called
because white men blackened their faces with burnt cork in
impersonation of negro characters and shows were based upon
life among the plantation negroes of the South.

The origin of negro minstrelsy is still hotly dis-
puted. Most plausible is the theory that it resulted from efforts of theatrical entertainers to duplicate the success of
Mr. Thomas D. Rice. Rice, an actor affectionately known as
"Daddy," became rich and famous through his singing and dancing characterization of "Jim Crowe." Crowe is said to have
been:

> "An old slave, whose name was Jim and who had
> adopted the family name of his master, there-
> after being known as Jim Crowe. Sadly deformed,
> his right knee was drawn high, his left leg
> stiff and crooked at the knee. The result was
> a painful and hideous limp. Dressed in ragged,
> ancient garments he sang an old tune and at the
> end of each verse he forced his grotesque limbs
> into a step known as 'rockin de wheel.'"

The description of "Jim Crowe" is based upon the
remembrances of Edmond S. Connor who met Rice who was performing his characterization at the Columbia Street Theatre,
Cincinnati, about 1828. Rice was sensational in the part, and
once negro impersonations had begun groups soon formed, not-
ably in Philadelphia and New York. By 1844 established minstrel shows were travelling through the Eastern states and
England.

Word must have drifted east that these scratch companies had struck "pay dirt" for other troupes soon followed.
Braving the frontier was typical of the venturesome, nomadic
spirit of the early minstrel. Important pioneer companies
were booked into San Francisco on the following schedule:

```
        Virginia Minstrels..Feb.9,1850..Washington Hall
        Sable Harmonists...Jan.15,1851...1st Jenny Lind
        Buckley's New Orleans
          Serenaders........Feb.2,1852......Armory Hall
        Ranier & Donaldson's
          Minstrels.........Mar.1,1852.....1st American
        Campbell's Minstrels..Nov.15,1852 ...Armory Hall
        Tracey's Minstrels..July 11,1853........Adelphi
        Donnelly's Minstrels..Sept.21,1853......Adelphi
        Backus San Francisco
          Minstrels.........Jan.24,1853......S. F. Hall
```

Such were the musical missionaries who introduced
and developed this new art to serve as a field of entertainment on the Pacific Coast for half a century. (For Minstrel
Troupes, see Appendix G.)

SOME FAMOUS PIONEER MINSTRELS

Modern minstrels such as Al Jolson and Eddie Cantor
had their counter-parts in the fifties.

William Birch was a famous comedian and end man. Entering black face in 1844, he first appeared at Maguire's Opera House in 1851, and remained in San Francisco for six years. Between 1857 and 1862 he toured the nation with various troupes.

David S. Wambold began his career in 1849. He first sang here at Hope Chapel in 1853 with Donaldson's Minstrels. Later he toured Europe with Brown and Templeton's Minstrels and appeared in England with the renowned Christy Troupe. Pauline Jacobson stated in the San Francisco Bulletin July 7, 1917:

> "David Wambold who played in the later Fifties and early Sixties was the highest priced balladist. His sweet, mellow tenor voice gained him $600 a week for a single song nightly, a high rate even for those days."

W. H. Bernard was the greatest Interlocutor. From Pauline Jacobson, the San Francisco Bulletin July 7, 1917:

> "Bernard, the pioneer middleman was appreciated by the end men for his large vocabulary (he had been educated as a lawyer) excellent for playing gags on."

Charles Backus, manager and comedian, gave great imitations of famous actors. He came to San Francisco in 1852 and shortly afterward organized the Backus Minstrels. He played in Australia (1855 and 1859), and travelled overland from there to England in 1860. Of this musical Marco Polo the Golden Era on January 29, 1854 reports:

> "The imitations by Backus are as wonderful as they are amusing. He is the ne plus ultra of delineation of negro characters."

Eph Horn was a capable "Bones," song and dance man, and female impersonator. He came here with the Christy Minstrels in 1854 after becoming nationally known for his cleverness and wit.

Billy Emerson, said to have been "the greatest minstrel who ever lived" and certainly the best of his time, entered minstrelsy in 1850. He did not appear here until 1870, after which time his success became legendary. San Franciscans of a later era said: "a minstrel show without Billy Emerson is like 'Hamlet' without the Danish Prince."

Other popular pioneer troubadors were:

```
Barker, William                               singer
Briggs, Tom                         famous Banjo player
          (died shortly after arrival)
Bryant, Jerry                               comedian
Buckley, S.                                   singer
Buckley, F.                                violinist
Campbell, L.                                  singer
Cotton, Ben     comedian, aged darky impersonator
Christy, George                   singer, comedian
De Angelis, John                            comedian
Henry, C.                                     singer
Rattler, Lew                comedian, impersonator
Wells, Sam                          excellent basso
Zorer, Max                      manager, impersonator
```

WHY MINSTRELS WERE POPULAR

The popularity of the minstrel can justly be attributed to the female sex. With exception of the rare occasions when Lotta Crabtree appeared in blackface, and perhaps one or two others, there were no women performers in minstrelsy. Double entendre jokes and gags, together with bawdy burlesque, played an important part but sex had a holiday. Yet women

were largely responsible for the success of the minstrel.
The following excerpt from an article by Pauline Jacobson,
published in the San Francisco Bulletin July 7, 1917 explains:

"After the excitement and hardships of the early
gold rush days life began to assume a more orderly, settled character in San Francisco. The
pioneer then wished for a congenial and refined
social life. For this the influence of women
was needed. This proved a definite problem.
There were few women in the city, of these many
disliked going to social functions, either
through lack of fine clothing or fear of ruin-
ing it as they walked through the muddy streets.
For a time men and women did meet at the concerts, operas, and operatic concerts provided
by Biscaccianti. Then the opera company left
and a decided slump was felt in San Francisco
social life. Wild enthusiasm greeted the minstrels at the opening performance. Nightly the
hall continued to be crowded. The hall became
a highly popular place of amusement where San
Francisco men regularly went, lessening their
visits to the saloons and gambling houses. The
problem of womens part in San Francisco society
had been settled. To the minstrel shows they
went, regardless of clothes or weather. By
1858 their attendance became so frequent, so
dependable that Jack Wilson at the Lyceum inaugurated the matinee. The minstrels attracted
the women, thus making the matinee, out of
which grew the matinee girl, creator of the
matinee idol and finally the great actors and
actresses which was later to make the California Theatre so famous."

There were other factors contributing to the success
of minstrels. Audiences liked the songs and music and were
delighted when "Bones" or "Tambo" bested the suave Interlocutor in verbal combat. Much credit is due Mr. Thomas Maguire
San Francisco's great impresario, for popularizing this type
of amusement. He brought the best minstrel talent here and
his efforts were to later bring the city honor and acclaim it

as a minstrel producing center. [1] Minstrels were popular "off stage" as well as "on"; they became a part of the growing city and took active interest in community life. On May 23, 1856 the San Francisco Bulletin recorded:

> "The San Francisco Minstrels, members of the theatrical profession, and the musical bands of the city with muffled instruments turned out for the funeral of James King of William the assasinated editor."

There were between seven and twelve men in the average troupe. The most important instrument was the banjo; typically negroid minstrel music from that of the ordinary theatre orchestra. Other instruments commonly played were violin, clarinet, cornet, horn, bass viol, and accordion. These were augmented by the use of novelty instruments such as combs, quills, jews'-harp, bag-pipes, tambourines, and bones.

In the latter fifties the parade was introduced and became a tradition. A polite form of bally-hoo advertised the show better than any other medium. Mr. E. B. Marks, who took part in many of these colorful events, describes the parade as follows:

> "The 11:45 parade, the boast and the curse of minstrel life was a thing of joy to the minstrels. Think of strutting down the main street in scarlet top-coat with brass buttons, or a plum-colored ulster with silver facings. The girls lined the curb. They had ample opportunity to observe each minstrel on their side of the street, for the parade consisted of two single files widely spaced, to make it seem bigger. In front blared a band composed of clarinet soloist, two bell ringers, a song and dance man doubling in brass and a few orchestra

---

1 See Tom Maguire, Volume 2, Theatre Research Series, O. P. 465-03-286.

fiddles ditto. Nothing ever sounded quite like
it! They sold their music to the crowd as they
would sell it to an audience in the theatre.
And the window panes rattled as they blew through
the streets."

THE SHOW: PART ONE

Part One consisted of a running dialogue between
the Interlocutor and the End Men, Bones and Tambo. The dialogue, always humorous, was regularly interrupted by set songs,
portentously announced by the Interlocutor. Part One ran
about as follows: [1]

> (As the curtain was drawn, the minstrels with
> blackened faces and comic clothing stood behind
> chairs arranged in a semi-circle, the Interlocu-
> tor stood in the exact center.)
>
> Inter: "Gentlemen be seated." (Chord in G ac-
> companied by tambourine.) "Well Mr. Bones, how
> are you feeling this evening?"
>
> **Bones:** "Very well Mr. Interlocutor, and how are
> you--how are all your folks?"
>
> Inter: "We're all well, exceptin' my brother.
> You see a team of horses ran away with him, and
> he's been laid up ever since."
>
> Bones: "That's a very strange coincidence,
> same thing happened to my brother."
>
> Inter: "You don't say."
>
> Bones: "The only difference is, it was my bro-
> ther who ran away with the team of horses; he's
> been laid up ever since, but they'll let him
> out next month."
>
> Inter: "My brother is convalescing, but we have
> to watch him closely--you see he's a somnambu-
> list, and he's liable to have a relapse."

---

1 Spaeth, Sigmund and Dailey Paskam. Gentlemen Be Seated
(New York: Doubleday Doran Co., 1928).

Bones: "My goodness!   A slambulnalist--,hat's dat?"

Inter: "Not a slambulnalist,   a somnambulist-- one who walks in his sleep."

Bones: "Oh,   you   mean   a   policeman."   (All laugh.)

Inter: "Our silver-voiced tenor will now render that ever popular ballad of blessed memory-- My Old Kentucky Home."

or: "Our sweet singer of spiritual and secular ditties   will now   interpret--Ring Dat Golden Bell with the help of the chorus."

This procedure was repeated several times and Part One was concluded by the "Walk Around," described by Messrs. Spaeth and Paskman as follows:

"The final 'Walk Around' rises to a frenzied pandemonium of rhythmic sound. Bones and Tambo at an angle of forty-five degrees and holding their noise makers high in air, sustain the climax as long as body and soul can stand the strain. A final triumphant chord from the band and the curtain drops on first part."

The Olio was an interlude of vaudeville-like acts not requiring the full stage or company. It gave the stage hands ample time to set the scenery for Part Two and permitted the introduction of specialty acts, dances, instrumental solos, monologues, and burlesque stump speeches.

The second part of the minstrel show was usually a burlesque of an opera, play, song parody or political situation. Spontaneity was the key note and players were given a wide latitude in ad-libbing their lines.   "Box and Cox" an old English play was "africanized for the Christy Minstrels." Females were impersonated by "Wenches" and hilarious situations developed.

MELODIES BY STEPHEN FOSTER

The beloved Foster wrote some of his songs especially
for minstrel presentation. <u>Old Folks at Home</u> was written
for Christy's Minstrels and originally published under the
name of E. P. Christy. Foster's biographer, John Tasker
Howard, states in <u>Stephen Foster, America's Troubadour</u>:

> "Stephen's later association with minstrel shows
> came naturally to him for in his boyhood 'play-
> ing theatre' meant imitating the songs and an-
> tics of black face comedians. Stephen later
> came to be associated with the leading perform-
> ers of his day, but it was in childhood that he
> first showed his fascination for anything con-
> nected with the stage."

Black face songsters helped popularize his songs
and those of other composers. Mr. E. B. Marks,[1] states:

> "A hit of the New York Halls might not by the
> chance currents of individual booking, reach
> the Chicago stage for years. But one agency
> could make a song a national hit in a season--
> the minstrel show."

Early minstrel songs genuinely expressed the spirit
of the plantation negro at work or rest. Foster's talent was
peculiarly adapted to this type of composition. While many
songs were comic -- they were definitely songs of broken
hearts and blighted romance, aged mothers and dying brothers
that made the greatest hit.

Mr. E. B. Marks states:

> "But we owe minstrelsy one great boon--it was
> responsible for the greatest songs ever written
> by an American. Without the encouragement of
> minstrels and minstrelsy--Stephen Foster who
> was a person easily discouraged, might not have
> continued."

---

1 Marks, E. B. <u>They All Sang</u> (New York: Viking Press, 1935.)

Foster melodies popular during the Gold Rush era include: Oh Susanna, Old Folks at Home, Old Black Joe, Massa's in de Col Col Ground, My Old Kentucky Home, Nelly Was A Lady, Old Dog Tray, Uncle Ned, Gwine to Run All Night, Hard Times Come Again No More.

Other famous minstrel songs of pioneer days were:

Dixie - Composed for Bryant's Minstrels in 1860 by Dan Emmett.
Kingdom Come - by Henry C. Work, 1863.
Rock Me to Sleep Mother - by Ernest Leslie, 184?
Rocked in the Cradle of the Deep - by J. P. Knight, 1839.
Darling Nellie Gray - by B. R. Hanby.
Lilly Dale - by H. S. Thompson, 1852.
Nicodemus Johnson - by J. B. Murphy, 1855.
Jim Along Josey - author unknown, 1849.
Sally Come Up - Frederick Buckley, 1862.
Clare de Kitchen - by T. Rice
Gideon's Band - by C. R. Dodworth, 1861.
Jingle Bells - by J. Pierpont, 1859.
Carry Me Back to Ole Virginny - James A. Bland.
The Original Jim Crowe Song - by T. Rice, a verse of which follows:

> "Oh Jim Crowe's come to town
> As you all must know,
> An' he wheel about, he turn about,
> He do jis so,
> An ebry time he wheel about
> He jump Jim Crowe."

"THE GRAND DUTCH S"

Operas most frequently burlesqued in Part Two were the Bohemian Girl, La Sonnambula, William Tell, and Offenbach's The Grand Duchess, which was presented under the title Dutch S. Other burlesques and Parodies of Part Two were:

Rocked in the Cradle of the Deep..Locked in the Stable with the Sheep.
Damon and Pythias...The Executioner Outwitted.
Romeo and Juliet........ Roman Nose and Suet.
Hamlet..,.............Gimlet-Prince of Dunkirk.
Othello.............................Old Fellow.
Camille...............................Clam-Eel.
Macbeth.............................Bad Breath.

Often required to amuse the same audience night after night, players were kept busy devising new gags and re-
vising old ones. San Francisco pioneers did not mind hearing
their favorite songs repeated, but jokes, Olio acts, and burlesques had to be renewed constantly or the show might become
a "turkey."

THE WORLD'S MINSTREL HEADQUARTERS

In the latter fifties and early sixties the city
became the minstrel production center of the world. Companies
were organized here for tours of Australia and the Orient as
well as the interior of this country. One of the greatest
companies of all time originated here in 1864. Formed under
the title of the "Original San Francisco Minstrels" it was a
partnership between four of minstrelsy's greatest stars,
Birch, Wambold, Bernard and Backus. The company remained here
for nearly a year after organization, then began a long triumphant engagement in New York where they were a smash hit.

Pioneer San Francisco did much for the minstrels
and vice versa. Besides gratifying an amusement loving
citizenry, and helping the enrichment of the new city's social life, the popular art contributed to the nation's diversified culture. [1]

---

1 See Minstrelsy, Vols. XIV and XV, S. F. Theatre Research
Project, O. P. 465-03-286.

GLOSSARY

Bones: End man, comedian. Also two dried bones rattled in hands like castanets.

End Man: Comedian, usually called Bones or Tambo.

Interlocutor: Master of ceremonies, foil for comedians.

Olio: An interlude of vaudeville acts between Part One and Part Two.

Rockin' de wheel: A minstrel dance step originated by Jim Crowe.

Tambo: End man, comedian.

Walk Around: Stage routine, finale of Part One.

Wench: Term for female impersonator.

JENNY LIND THEATRE.

SATURDAY EVENING, JUNE 26th, 1852.

A GRAND CONCERT

WILL BE GIVEN AT THE ABOVE NAMED TIME AND PLACE, BY THE ORIGINAL

NEW ORLEANS SERENADERS,

COMPLIMENTARY

TO THE LATE MANAGER, HENRY B PLATT.

First Night of the Laughable Burlesque on the Rainer Family !

Burlesque Violin Solo · · · · by POMPEY.

Dress Circle.................\$2 00 | Parquette....................\$1 00
Second Tier..................1 00 | Gallery.......................50

Doors open at 7½ o'clock—Concert to commence at 8½ o'clock.

Seats can be secured at Atwill's Music Store, and at Marvin & Hitchcock's, during the day.

PART FIRST.

AS DANDY DARKIES OF THE NORTH.

Ethiopian Gallop, (composed by F. Buckley.)..................COMPANY.
Operatic Chorus...COMPANY.
A Little More Cider.....................................G. SWAINE BUCKLEY.
The Old Pine Tree...J. H. COLLINS.
Nancy Till...R. BISHOP BUCKLEY.
Jolly Old Crow..J. H. COLLINS.
Bone Solo.—Imitation of Drums and Military Training.....G. SWAINE BUCKLEY.
Old Folks at Home, (by particular desire).....................J. H. COLLINS.
Laughing Chorus...G. SWAINE BUCKLEY.
Congaloe Fox Hunt..COMPANY.

Grand Burlesque on the Musical Panorama, introducing

THE HORNS

WITH FEATURES ORIGINAL WITH THIS COMPANY.
The effect in this splendid composition is left entirely to the imagination of the audience.

PART SECOND.

Violin Solo—Descriptive of a Bird that has escaped from his cage, and hopping from tree to tree attempts to sing the favorite airs taught to it by the Mistress...F. BUCKLEY.
Double Tambourine Dance....................G. S. BUCKLEY AND MULLEN.
Favorite Ballad — Then You'll Remember me...................J. H. COLLINS.
Banjo Solo...G. SWAINE BUCKLEY.
Banjo Trio — Sandy Point, (first time,) the...........BUCKLEYS AND BARRY
Bellows Solo..G. SWAINE BUCKLEY.
Highland Fling...J. J. MULLEN.

GRAND BURLESQUE ON THE

ITALIAN OPERA SINGERS!

Violin Solo......................THE DREAM.................F. BUCKLEY.

BURLESQUE TYROLEAN - - - A LA RAINER.

Dance, Fanny Bloomer.......................................J. J. MULLEN.
Burlesque Violin Solo....................................E. BISHOP BUCKLEY.
Sally White...J. H. COLLINS.
Camptown Races, (with imitation of horse-racing,)........G. SWAINE BUCKLEY.
Good-Bye Sally, Dear.....................................R. BISHOP BUCKLEY.
Statue Dance, with Local Hits, - - - - J. J. Mullen and Buckley.

[FRANKLIN PRESS, MONTGOMERY STREET.]

SAN FRANCISCO, July 23d, 1852.

To MR. HENRY B. PLATT.

SIR: For your courtesy and gentlemanly management, while acting as Director of Buckley's New Orleans Serenaders, and the able and efficient manner in which you have enabled us to earn an enviable reputation, we, in common with our fellow-citizens, beg leave most respectfully to tender you a Benefit, and ask that you may name a night when most convenient for you, that we may show you that worth to which you are held, and a testimonial to your merits, of which you may justly feel proud.

We are

Very respectfully,

R. BISHOP BUCKLEY,   F. BUCKLEY,   J. J. MULLEN,
G. SWAINE BUCKLEY,   J. H. COLLINS,   A. H. BARRY.

S. R. HARRIS, Mayor,   Hon. J. C. HAYS, Sheriff.   GEO. HOSSEFROSS, C. Engineer,
Alderman C. HYATT,   Judge SMITH,   Dr. NILES,
W. D. M. HOWARD,   JAMES WILDER,   T. K. BATTELLE,
Judge HUDENPELT,   W. CROWELL,   J. W. GREGORY,
Judge SHEPARD,   J. E. WAINWRIGHT, J. W. STILLMAN,
Judge MORRIS,   Dr. LAMPTE,   J. L. PENDLETON.

SAN FRANCISCO, June 24, 1852.

To the MESSRS. BUCKLEY,

HON. S. R. HARRIS, J. C. HAYS, GEO. HOSSEFROSS, &c.:—

Your note of the 22d inst., tendering me a Complimentary Benefit, is before me. For the kind and generous terms in which you are pleased to speak of, and the flattering compliment offered me, I am unaffectedly grateful, and trust that I may ever be worthy of the friendship and high regard in which it is my good fortune to be held by you.

In retiring from the management of the justly celebrated Company of New Orleans Serenaders, I beg to tender them my hearty thanks for the unvarying courtesy extended towards me at all times, and hope that their prosperity may be commensurate with my wishes for their welfare.

I would respectfully suggest the night of SATURDAY, JUNE 26TH, as a suitable occasion for the proposed Benefit, if it suits your accommodation.

With sincere gratitude and profound regard,

I am, Gentlemen,

Yours, &c.,

HENRY B. PLATT.

CHAPTER TEN: THE HEYDAY OF GRAND OPERA

o sooner had Italian grand opera attained a footing in America than it was transplanted across the continent to San Francisco. Soon no city in America was more eager to hear the latest importation from Italy; company after company trekked to the turbulent city by the Golden Gate.

Operatic selections formed a large part of the earliest concerts in 1850, and in January of the following year grand opera made its debut. From that day on grand opera rode a crest of popularity which was diminished only by the empty pockets of the '70's and the sweeping advent of light opera at the Tivoli Gardens.

Grand opera seemed peculiarly suited to the tempo of life in the early days. Drama and passion were in the very atmosphere. Fortunes were made and lost overnight. Vigilantes banded together to preserve law and order. The entertainment of such a community had to match the intense and almost melodramatic mode of daily life. The newly rich were hungry for the grandiose.

A contemporary newspaperman, with far-reaching vision, editorializes thus in the <u>Daily Alta California</u> of April 25, 1853, under the heading "Musical":

"There are probably few cities in the world, or any of its population, that affords so liberal a support to the same number of artists, of every class and order, as San Francisco. From the 'first fiddle' of Miska Hauser, through all the gradations of talent and skill, down to the lazy organ grinders who perambulate our streets from morning till night; from the charming prima donnas, Biscaccianti and Hayes, down to Mary, the accordion girl, who sings in the saloons and cafes; all meet with a generous reward for their performances. For months Mme. Biscaccianti sang to admiring audiences; Miss Hayes has given series after series of concerts, with signal success; Miska Hauser's bow, like the wand of a magician, excites to raptures large and fashionable audiences; the concerts of the Alleghanians are pleasantly remembered by hundreds of our citizens; company after company of Serenaders have tarried with us from time to time, contributing much to the amusement of our citizens, and to their own profit; our saloons and theatres support many excellent orchestras; we can boast of some fine instrumental bands, who, almost daily, head processions through our streets; these, together with a host of small fry, who pick up a living from door to door, making both day and night hideous with their dolorous bellowings, prove beyond a doubt that the people of San Francisco--comprising, as they do, specimens of almost every class of nearly every nation upon the globe, even to the four castes of China--appreciate and reward musical talent according to its various degrees of merit.

"What other city, outside of California, pays two or three thousand dollars for a day's professional music? In what other city does the player upon the clarionet or trombone command fifty dollars for blowing about the streets during a day's parade? Under such favorable circumstances, why is there not a movement made to establish here an operatic troupe of the first class, by subscriptions or otherwise?

That Signor Biscaccianti made such a proposition
some months since, we are aware; but why he was
not successful or why the matter should have
been allowed to drop, we are not informed. We
feel assured, however, that if properly taken
in hand, this object could be accomplished, and
would prove highly profitable to those who un-
dertake the task. In the absence of Barnum who
will take the first step?"

THE FIRST OPERA SEASON

Already in 1851 there were regular performances of
French and Italian opera. The first to arrive was the "Pellegrini Italian Opera Troupe" and the performance given
should have rightly been called an "Operatic Concert." Their
ambitious plan to present Bellini's La Sonnambula could not be
perfected on such short notice, and the program consisted
merely of selections from that opera. In addition to the local talent enlisted for this concert, there was also a dancing
team, as is stated in the report that "The Lorentes were excellent in their character dances, and added much to the evening's entertainment." The event took place at the Adelphi
Theatre on Friday evening, January 24, 1851, and tickets sold
for one to four dollars. According to the review in the next
day's Daily Alta California:

> "It was well attended and appeared to render
> good satisfaction to the audience. We under-
> stand that it is the intention of the director,
> Sig. T. Pellegrini, to make such additions to
> his company as will enable him to produce grand
> operas in the style they require, and we hope
> that our musical amateurs, by their patronage,
> will enable him to carry out his designs. The

prima donna, Signora Mauri, made a most favorable impression and, in conjunction with Signor
Pellegrini, received a most flattering amount
of applause. It is understood that there will
be a performance, in the course of a few evenings, at which time the entire opera 'La Sonnambula' will be given."

Two weeks later this promise was kept, and in the
fort-night to follow, it was presented four times. Norma was
given February 27 and the day following the paper stated that
"the house was literally crowded last evening by a fashionable audience to hear Bellini's opera Norma." Ernani was announced for March 28 but was postponed until April 8 because
of Madam Von Gulpen's sudden and unexplained departure for
Sacramento. The last night was a benefit for Signor Pellegrini.
The Troupe was composed of Signore Abalos and Rosina Mauri
(Pellegrini), Mme. Von Gulpen, and Signori Innocenzo Pellegrini, Acquasoni, Guinde, and Roncovieri. (For Opera, see Appendix F.)

The last mentioned was Count Alfred Pierre Roncovieri, basso-cantante of the Grand Opera of Bordeaux, France,
who made his debut in San Francisco as assisting artist with
Henri Herz on April 2, 1850. He appeared often accompanied
by his wife in many of the French and Italian operas played
during the seasons of 1850 to 1873, and sang with the Pellegrini, Bianchi, Ghioni, Richings, Bishop, Bonheur, Lyster,
and Agatha States opera companies. [1]

---

1 Above information supplied by singer's son, Alfred Roncovieri, present City Supervisor.

A GREAT TRIUMVIRATE

Eliza Biscaccianti

A triumvirate of great prima donnas, -- Eliza Biscaccianti, Catherine Hayes, and Madam Bishop -- fittingly laid the foundation of San Francisco's interest in good music and good voices. The first to arrive was Eliza Biscaccianti, and in February of 1852 she was a pioneer indeed, venturing into a musical wilderness which P. T. Barnum did not dare to risk with Jenny Lind and Kate Hayes. This small, dainty, bird-like singer succeeded overnight in bettering the social aspects of a crude and unpolished frontier town. For the men in the audience -- whether miner in rough flannel shirt or gentleman gambler in frilled linen -- she embodied grace, domestic joys and refinements long since abandoned.

Mme. Biscaccianti inaugurated her first opera season March 22, 1852, at the American Theatre. When the date was announced the demand for carriages far exceeded the supply. The Grace Episcopal Church on Powell Street was to have been the scene of this concert, but the demand for tickets was so great that the performance had to be removed to the American Theatre. The Daily Alta California, two days later describes the effect of the epoch making concert in these words:

> "The next day the people went about in a daze and even the most sober minded and judicial subscribed to the decision of the press that the evening marked an era in the musical, social and fashionable progress of the city."

EARLY OPERA PROGRAMS

The program which set the style for all future measures of excellence in the minds of San Franciscans was as
follows: Recitative and aria from Donizetti's Linda di Chamounix, Ad tardai troppo, and Oh luce di quest anima, English
ballad, Neapolitaine, I am Dreaming of Thee, Home Sweet Home,
Meyerbeer's Robert le Diable, Robert, toi que j'aime, The
Last Rose of Summer, Bellini's La Sonnambula, Ah non Guinze.

From the above program it is again seen that opera
or rather the operatic concert, in those earliest times often
consisted largely of excerpts, often from several operas. The
reasons for this are found in the lack of adequate scenery,
costumes and supporting chorus groups. Another fact is that
audiences were unfamiliar with opera librettos, and appreciated a well sung ballad more than the narrative recitative
which carried the story of the music drama. There was, however, some semblances of presenting an opera, and Biscaccianti, like Pellegrini, enlisted the best local talent available
to support her. Among these artists were Miss Emelie Coad,
Mme. Foubert, Signor Moretto, and Monsieur Coulon. A nearer
approach to opera was found in the operatic costume concerts
of Biscaccianti's rival Kate Hayes who was soon to appear.

Other appearances followed with the same enthusiastic receptions. According to the Daily Alta California of
March 31, 1852:

> "The American Theatre was filled again last eve-
> ning on the occasion of Mme. Biscaccianti's

second concert. The program was new, with the
exception of the finale to 'La Sonnambula.' On
March 27, at her third concert, she sang the
Cavatina from 'Ernani' gems from 'Lucia' and
'Comin' Thru the Rye.' On March 29, the orchestra, under the leadership of George Loder, gave
two excellent overtures. Monsieur Coulon gave
the recitative and aria from Adams' 'Le Chalet'
and Rossini's 'La Gloire.' Mme. Biscaccianti
sang 'I am Queen of a Fairy Band,' Casta Diva
from 'Norma,' and 'Oh Cast That Shadow from My
Brow.'"

On July 3 the Daily Alta California reports that she

sang John Anderson, My Jo, Believe Me If All Those Endearing

Young Charms, Porgi Amor by Mozart, and scenes from La Son-

nambula. "The approbation of the public knew no bounds and a

shower of bravos and bouquets greeted the conclusion."

These public approbations were stimulated in no

small way by the numerous benefit performances and generous

gifts of the young prima donna to churches and other institu-

tions which had been ravaged by fires that so often visited the

the city in its early days. At a benefit concert, at the

Grace Episcopal Church, Mme. Biscaccianti gave Rossini's Sta-

bat Mater. Fire companies came out in full uniform to honor

her, and on one occasion their enthusiasm was so great that

they unhitched the horses from her carriage and pulled it to

her hotel.

Several trips to San Jose, Sacramento, and Marys-

ville followed, and later another series of ten concerts were

given at the Jenny Lind Theatre. Meanwhile, Catherine Hayes

had arrived and between the two a jealousy arose which was

fostered mainly by the two newspapers and the following each prima donna had among the citizenry. The furore aroused eventually led to the premature departure of Biscaccianti   for South America in February of 1853. After   nearly a year in California she left for Lima, Peru, and from thence   went on a world tour. Altogether she had given seventy-one   performances in California and had earned a small fortune.

Six years later she returned to find that the frontier town of tents and shacks had grown to a metropolis second only to New York in theatrical importance. But San Francisco had forgotten Biscaccianti; there were too many other attractions. For a time she sang with the Lyster Company, usurping the place of Lucy Escott. That company soon left for Australia but Biscaccianti remained and many misfortunes remained with her. Eventually she took to drink, spent several years singing in the fetid air of the Bella Union, and finally mustering all her courage went to Lima, Peru, where she made a splendid comeback.

KATE HAYES

Soon after Biscaccianti left in 1853 her place in the public's affection was usurped by Kate Hayes, the "Swan of Erin." Hayes, according to the discerning, was simply a ballad singer without the voice or style or culture of Biscaccianti. But these failings were silenced by the louder voice of her press agent.

To prevent speculation in tickets the agents decided that it would be best to place the tickets at auction, a quaint custom but fairly frequent in this period. Bidding started at $50 and choice seats brought, in one instance, the sum of $1,150 paid for by the Empire Fire Engine Company. Sacramento, not to be outdone, paid $1200 for a single ticket.

On the evening of November 30, 1852, Catherine Hayes stepped on the platform of the American Theatre and faced a house crowded with the wealth and beauty of the city. The morning after the concert, the critic of the Daily Alta California reports:

> "Long and loud were the cheers which greeted her entree. Silence having been restored, Miss Hayes sang the sweet and plaintive invocation, 'Ah, mon fils!' one of the most touching gems of Meyerbeer's music. Her voice is naturally mezzo-soprano. Excessive study has forced it perhaps a shade higher. It is sweet, mellow, lacking, if anything, power. In the upper register her notes certainly require strength. Her voice is admirably cultivated, flexible, and the delightful shake or quaver which she introduces with so much effect, imparts a softness or tremulousness to her plaintive songs, soothing or agreeable to the listener.
>
> "Miss Hayes was ably assisted in the duet from 'Norma' by Herr Mengis, baritone. Previous to this duetto, Signor Herold executed a fantasia on the piano with much taste and skill.
>
> "Altogether the concert was highly successful. There was much enthusiasm and altogether too much noise and uproariousness. Some younger sons of Erin became so much excited as to toss hats and money upon the stage, which however enthusiastic it may seem, could not but be regarded as extremely bad taste.
>
> "The program also contained an interpretation of 'The Last Rose of Summer' a scene from 'Don Pasquale' and several ballads.

"Her ballads being the most exquisitely rendered were repeatedly encored. At the close Miss
Hayes was escorted to the Oriental Hotel by a
torchlight procession composed of a body of our
firemen, and serenaded."

Much controversy was rampant concerning the merits
of Hayes and Biscaccianti, the result of which is that excellent criticisms of both appear. It may be that Biscaccianti
had the edge in these arguments, for some hinted that Hayes'
success was due more to her personality than to her voice.
Also resented was her financial success, and a critic in the
Golden Era of February 13, 1853 is somewhat malicious about
her concerts in the Grass Valley region: "It is stated that
Kate Hayes has been mining. That is, after the miners had
dug and washed the precious ore, she, with characteristic
shrewdness, picked out the big lumps."

OPERALOGUES

Giving entire concerts in concert form, Miss Hayes
began a series of costume recitals on December 23, 1852.
Among these were The Barber of Seville, Lucia, Don Pasquale,
Norma, Elisir d'Amore, Linda, Lucrezia Borgia and The Daughter
of the Regiment. These were a continuous artistic and financial success and by the middle of March 1853, she had given
thirty-seven concerts. Prices for these costume recitals of
complete operas were $5, $3 and $2. They were given under
the musical direction of George Loder, with only the assistance of Herr Mengis, baritone, and Miss Coad, soprano. There

was no chorus, no scenery of any magnitude, no orchestra
of operatic size. Kate Hayes evidently travelled light and
kept the profit for herself.

A fine summary of her San Francisco activities is
found in the Daily Alta California of May 15, 1853, in which
the critic praises her success but avoids much comment on her
ability:

> "The Firemen's Testimonial to Miss Hayes.--The
> complimentary benefit tendered Miss Hayes by
> the Fire Department of San Francisco, took place
> last night before an equally large and brilliant
> audience which filled the theatre the evening
> previous. The Fire Department turned out in
> large numbers in uniform; the theatre was dec-
> orated with the insignia of service and the
> greatest enthusiasm seemed to prevail. Miss
> Hayes looked well and sang well. Among the
> pieces there was an original composition en-
> titled a 'Farewell to California.' It poss-
> essed no striking merit. At the conclusion of
> the concert she was saluted by hearty cheers to
> which she returned a few appropriate remarks.
> She was afterward escorted to her hotel by the
> companies, and there also she was complimented
> by cheers, huzzas and the waving of torches.
> She retired amid much enthusiasm and was evident-
> ly deeply impressed with the closing ceremonies
> of her California career...Whatever reputation
> she may have acquired in other countries in no
> part of the world has Miss Hayes been so suc-
> cessful as in California. Her concerts -- some
> forty or fifty since her arrival on our shores--
> have netted her nearly $30,000.
>
> "Though the reputation which was kindled for
> Miss Hayes on her arrival here, it was very soon
> ascertained by sensible men, was greater than
> her merit as an artist would justify, it did
> not detract from her success, as evidence of
> the liberality and whole-souled friendliness of
> our citizens..."

After this departure, Miss Hayes went to South America where she was well received. The following year she returned for a three month's stay but, unlike Biscaccianti, was as well received as she had formerly been. On April 24, 1854, she reappeared in Norma at the Metropolitan. On July 7, 1854 she gave a farewell concert and left for Australia the next day.

ANNA BISHOP

The third great prima donna to appear in San Francisco during the gold rush decade was Anna Bishop. She had an unusually eventful life and her biography has the elements of a popular novel. She was the inspiration for "Trilby," Du Maurier's best seller, it is reported; and the hypnotic influence exercised over her by the famous harpist of the day, Signor Bochsa supplied a theme for legends. Bochsa accompanied her to San Francisco where he became musical director of the Metropolitan.

She made her concert debut February 7, 1854, at the Musical Hall on Bush Street near Montgomery Street, and her first operatic appearance was in Norma which opened at the Metropolitan April 30, 1854. This was followed by the popular La Sonnambula and Don Pasquale. Some of the better received operas which she gave included Martha, Lucrezia Borgia, Lucia di Lammermoor, La Favorita, Amelia, and the Biblical opera Judith. On August 10, when she gave Der Freischütz in German at the Turnverein Hall, the gas went out and the audience went home.

In addition to opera she gave the oratorios, <u>The</u> <u>Creation</u> and <u>Stabat Mater</u>. In the nearly two years of her residence here she had given, according to <u>McCabe's Journal</u> forty operas, twenty-four benefit concerts, four oratorios, and seven Sunday concerts at Turnverein Hall.

<u>Robert the Devil</u> was reviewed in <u>The Golden West</u> on February 11, 1855, as follows:

> "On Sunday this theatre was filled by the music lovers among the foreign population, drawn together by the representation of 'Robert le Diable.' Mme. Bishop as the Countess and Alice sang splendidly. In 'Robert toi que j'aime,' she created a furore, in accomplishing which, Bochsa's masterly accompaniment on the harp had no small share.
>
> "That the enthusiasm exhibited by the audience, so different from the comparatively cool reception given to talent even when fully appreciated by an American assemblage, had something to do with it, is not unlikely. Roncovieri, as Bertram, exhibited power which he had not hitherto manifested..."

A more critical view of Madam Bishop is found in the <u>Pioneer Magazine</u>, in which an interesting comparison between Bishop and Hayes is found:

> "Madam Bishop had a far superior voice to Thillon's, but inferior to Kate Hayes. In regards to grand opera, however, she was considered far superior...in the expression of high and lofty sentiments, emanating from a grand and noble character, we look for and expect a full powerful voice such as Madam Bishop possesses; and we are not satisfied with any art without this ...Notwithstanding the fact that **excellent** judges pronounce her a very superior artiste, the point seems to be settled that she cannot render herself popular among the masses of the community. Her houses were but moderate, although we are happy to say they were attended by those who could appreciate true excellence in art."

This is doubtlessly an accurate estimate of Madam Bishop. Reviews of her many concerts and operas speak of her excellence as an accomplished fact rather than with the riotous gusto of acclaim that greeted Hayes. Madam Bishop left for Australia in September of 1855, and it was ten years before she again returned to win more triumphs. Her last local appearance is described by the San Francisco Daily Herald of September 28, 1855:

> "Since the Hall of the Turnverein was built, it has never presented a more brilliant or more animated scene than it did last evening, on the occasion of the farewell benefit given to Madam Anna Bishop...The well thronged space and the enthusiastic applause which ever anon followed each effort of Madam Bishop, testified strongly as to the feeling evoked on the present occasion towards the gifted cantatrice...Madam Bishop sang in her best style, and all of her most successful as well as most beautiful solos were in turn given to the well pleased audience.....
> Taken all in all, whether as a musical performance or as a tribute to the genius and artistic powers of Madam Bishop, the affair was certainly in the highest degree meritorious, and the compliment paid the lady no more than a simple tribute to the worth and justice of her claims on the music loving community of San Francisco."

ANNA THILLON

The last of the great triumvirate was now gone, but there was a host of less important but nevertheless widely acclaimed prima donnas and opera companies also active at this time. Among these were Anna Thillon, the Bianchis and Signorina Brambilla. Anna Thillon arrived in San Francisco December 31, 1853, and sang regularly with the French Opera Company at the Metropolitan. During the spring of the next year she was heard in: <u>Crown Diamonds</u>, <u>The Daughter of the</u> <u>Regiment</u>, <u>Bohemian Girl</u>, <u>The Enchantress</u>, and <u>Cinderella</u>. Complaints were made in the <u>Pioneer</u> that Thillon was entirely too prominent, much to the detriment of the ensemble and the opera as a whole. The cast of <u>Cinderella</u> as of March 21, 1854, shows that several local persons were included:

```
"Cinderella....................Mme. Anna Thillon
Fairy Queen....................Miss Julia Gould
Clorinda.......................Miss Julia Pelby
Felix...............................Mr. Hudson
Baron Pompolina.....................Herr Mengis
Dandine................................Mr. Leach
```

N. B. Children in arms not admitted."

THE BIANCHIS

The Bianchis, Eugenio and Giovanna, were engaged by impresario Tom Maguire early in 1858, and remained for nearly ten years. During this decade they produced Italian Opera continuously and achieved a certain prestige by sheer force of momentum. San Francisco, lacking the presence of the great stars of a few years past, settled down to the conviction that the Bianchis would suffice until more prominent talent ventured out from the East.

The Bianchis did not remain long under Tom Maguire. They cancelled their contract with him and set up an opera troupe independently at the American Theatre. This company, at various times, included Elvira Brambilla, Eliza Biscaccianti, Mme. Kleba, and Messrs. Gregg, Miller, Roncovieri, Leach and Kleba. One new opera which the Bianchis introduced was <u>Il Trovatore</u>. A lengthy review in the <u>Daily Bulletin</u> of

May 6, 1859, is very enlightening on a number of points:

> "'Il Trovatore,' for a first performance, was
> last night a great success. Italian opera here
> has many disadvantages to contend against. Gen-
> erally speaking, it is impossible to muster a
> chorus of female voices; then, the chorus of
> male voices is German, while the principal solo
> singers are Italian, French, German, Spanish or
> English, as the good fortune of the time may
> have it, while all are mingled together in the
> same piece. Again, while the orchestra players
> in this city are indeed excellent musicians they
> seldom perform in large numbers together, and
> from want of constant practice, cannot give that
> nicety and completeness of harmonious action
> that distinguished the operatic orchestras of
> the great cities of Europe and the United States.
> It is true, however, that we do not expect here
> that exquisite tout-ensemble of Italian opera
> that marks those places, and are satisfied with
> a much less approach to perfection. A very hun-
> gry man is not fastidious as to the character
> of the victuals that satisfy his appetite.   So
> here, we have been so long without dramatic
> music of the highest class, that we are prepared
> to make every allowance for shortcomings and
> rejoice in the feast as it is set before us.
>
> "The plot of 'Il Trovatore' was sufficiently
> told in our columns yesterday. Signora Bianchi,
> as 'Leonora' has the great work of the piece
> before her, and she performed it effectively.
> Her voice is not the most soft and sympathetic
> in the world, yet it is powerful and skill-
> fully managed, and with her passionate articu-
> lation served to carry the audience enthusiasti-
> cally with her. Mme. Feret, with a voice of
> less volume, is an exceedingly sweet and pleas-
> ing singer. Her tones, clear, soft and sympathet-
> ic, charm the hearer, while her acting is en-
> titled to very high praise...The 'Manrico' of
> Signor Bianchi, was nothing as a piece of act-
> ing. This gentleman is somewhat clumsy in his
> stage attitudes and movements, and he (and the
> same remark may be applied to Signora Bianchi)
> has little expression in his countenance; yet
> his singing is very fine, and always gives much
> delight to his audience...

"With good taste, the members of the orchestra paid some attention to their costumes, as all had on white vests except one grim old Frenchman. He might have dispensed with his dingy waistcoat altogether, and a reasonable clean shirt would have been a substitute not noticed for the white chest of his brethren....

"We may add, that the costumes, scenery and stage appointments generally, were of a magnificent description;...an improvement would be effected by dispensing with the cow-bell used to signal the orchestra into their places, preparatory to calling up the curtain..."

The San Francisco Bulletin, May 20, 1859:

"'Ernani' was produced last night to a numerous audience. A large portion of the music is so beautiful that even indifferently rendered it is sure to please. The want of a female chorus is still more felt here than in the case of 'Il Trovatore.' The eight German voices that form the chorus are powerful enough for the small house, but they are coarse; and the audience long in vain for the variety and sweetness of female voices. As it is, there is a monotony and harshness in the chorus that is very, very far from giving one a true idea of Italian opera. We trust that the new English opera troupe will bear this in mind, and at whatever cost, continue to produce at least half a dozen female choristers in their pieces. The Barili-Thorne Troupe of 1854-1855 managed to bring out that moderate number."

MINOR PERSONALITIES

There were many less talented persons of the concert and operatic stage who came to San Francisco during the first decade, remained for a season or two, and left for other places of employment. Among these may be mentioned Signora Abalos, Madam Barili-Thorne, Madam Cailly, Signora Garbato, Miss Lizzie Parker, Madam Agatha States, and Madam Von Gulpen.

Italian grand opera had its heyday during the fifties and sixties because, to the city by the Golden Gate, it

represented culture and refinement, and its grandiose, melodramatic passions found a responsive chord in the tempo
of everyday life. In a later decade this instinctive desire
for the flamboyant had worn itself out. When the tastes of
the populace of San Francisco demanded a lighter, more humorous touch, the time was propitious for the advent of the Tivoli Opera House where laughter and the land of make-believe
held the spotlight. [1]

---

[1] See, History of Opera in San Francisco Vols. VII and VIII,
pub. by San Francisco Theatre Research Project, O.P.465-03-286.

CHAPTER ELEVEN: VISITING VIRTUOSI

HENRI HERZ (1806--1888)

he world-famous prima donnas, Hayes, Bis-
caccianti, and Bishop were not the   only
artists who came to El Dorado during the
Gold Rush era. There also came   instrumentalists of renown such as Herz, Hauser,
Bochsa, Strakosch and Ole Bull.

First among the celebrities to heed the call of art
for gold's sake was the eminent pianist-composer, Henri Herz.
He was born in Vienna, January 6, 1806. His father was an
instructor in pianoforte in Vienna, and with him Henri began
the study of piano. After a short time the family moved to
Goblentz where the boy studied with Huten. His first public
performance was a concert when he was but eight years of age.
Henri was heralded as a child prodigy, but when his left hand
became weakened his father urged him to study the violin.

In April, 1816 Henri Herz entered the Conservatoire
in Paris as a pupil of Pradher. During the first year, Herz
won first prize in pianoforte, playing the difficult compositions of Daurhen. He remained in Paris several years. In 1821
he returned to the Conservatoire to resume his study and improve his style of playing.

Ten years elapsed before Henri Herz actually began his public life. In 1831 he made a tour of Germany and was received with only a mild response. Three years later he ventured into England where he played duets with such renowned artists as Ignaz Moscheles and J. B. Cramer.

Like many artists, Herz was an exceptionally poor business man. A short time before his London visit he had invested his fortune in a pianoforte factory with a man named Klepfer. Evidently Mr. Klepfer was a versatile salesman with many get-rich-quick schemes, and the result was that Klepfer absconded with the money. However, it took more than the loss of a few thousand francs to convince Henri Herz that his ability as a manufacturer was nil. He determined to own a factory of his own, but the urgent need was money. With this goal in view he planned a concert tour of America to recoup his fortune.

GO WEST YOUNG MAN

Toward the end of February 1850 people were dreaming of but one thing -- gold mines and California. Henri Herz, inflicted with the fever, joined a ship-load of adventurers, California bound. After the many inconveniences attendant on a long voyage on a crowded little ship, Herz entered the port of San Francisco. He felt himself somewhat recompensed for all his hardships by the novelty of the scene.

He found himself in a new town where most of the streets were impassable, and a pedestrian often had to wade in

mud up to his knees. Side-walks were insecure constructions
of planks, empty boxes and barrels nailed together.

His problem was to convey his piano, shipped from
the East, to the theatre. As he passed by a cafe he inquired
where he could find someone to take over the task of moving.
Two obliging gentlemen offered their services and   carried
the instrument to the theatre. Mr. Herz was less distracted
by the exorbitant price of three hundred dollars than by the
fact that the men posed as kindly gentlemen when they were
mere porters!

The next work was to find an orchestra. This was
a problem. There were unemployed musicians of all kinds , o-
pen however to such objections as blindness on the part of the
clarinet player, incurable asthma on that of the cornet player, etc., Herz promised to hire them for some future engagement.

He then requested a friend to conduct him to the
office of the principal journal in order to publish the necessary announcement. The office of the paper was on the
ground floor of a two story building. Two large dogs refused
to let them pass until appeased by a negress who conducted
the men into the presence of the editor. He was a tall, athletic individual with a beard, a red shirt, a large pair of
hunting boots, and an acute twitching of the right eye. He
wrote, sitting at a desk with a cudgel and a brace of pistols
beside him.

The visitors were informed that they might advertise the concert for the small sum of four dollars per line. Henri Herz paused a moment, looked at the uncompromising aspect of the editor, at the pistols and paid the price.

The day of the concert arrived, and at an early hour the theatre was besieged by fierce, rough-looking creatures who were deeply offended if they were offered second-rate seats at four dollars. The public filed past the money-taker, and each in turn placed his hand in a black leather purse and drew forth a pinch of gold dust. This was weighed and, if satisfactory, the individual was given a ticket.

The concert from an artistic point of view was a failure because the confusion and boisterious conduct of the audience made it impossible for the artist to be appreciated. In a stage box, Herz recognized three ladies, one who had been the keeper of a small shop in Paris, and two French milliners who had retired from business. They were living in the style and luxury to which they felt they should have been accustomed. One of the ladies had posed as a duchess.

Much to his surprise, at the conclusion of the concert, Mr. Herz was given a pan filled with gold dust amounting to something like ten thousand francs. Henri Herz gave fourteen concerts in the same manner, with the same success and the same profit. He began to be reconciled to San Francisco.

On one occasion a gentleman approached him with the offer of an engagement in "a private gambling and pleasure

house."   Henri's dignity was offended, and he proceeded to
usher the gentleman out by physical force.

FLOATING A GRAND PIANO

After fourteen concerts Herz decided that he would
get some of the gold first handed. He found conditions in
the gold mines unbearable and soon discovered that his gold
was to be found in the keys of a piano. He journeyed to Sacramento where he designed the plans for a music hall. Within
a fort-night the building was completed and the artist was
ready to win a new audience. The miners had paid liberally
for the concert. According to the Dramatic Chronicle, May 25,
1867 the following incident occurred:

> "At the hour announced for the concert, the
> tickets were all sold, the house was crowded,
> the artist was at his post, and everything in
> readiness except the piano. In consequence of
> the inexplicable delay, the instrument had not
> yet arrived. Herz looked at his rough and
> bearded auditory in a very agreeable trepida-
> tion. What if the gold digging dilettanti
> should take it into their heads to give him a
> taste of revolver or bowie knife, by the way of
> filling up the time? Heavy drops of perspira-
> tion stood on the frightened pianists brow, and
> he began to wish himself in China, or anywhere
> but California. The miners saw his alarm and
> kindly comforted him. 'Never mind the cussed
> piano,' said two or three of them soothingly,
> 'we don't care for it; we came to see you. Make
> us a speech.' Herz restored to serenity did
> the best he could. The spoken entertainment
> seemed to please the audience; and everybody,
> except the artist, had quite forgotten all about
> the piano, when its arrival was announced. A
> number of strong men carried the instrument in-
> to the hall, and placed it on the platform. It
> was a three cornered, or 'grand' piano, and
> Herz, promising himself to astonish these simple

and easily satisfied inhabitants of the Pacific Coast, seated himself on an empty whiskey keg (instead of the more civilized stool) and ran his fingers over the key board. Blum! Blum! splash! splash! not a sound did the piano utter, save that of the keys striking the water. The Californians, who had brought the box from San Francisco, finding it very heavy, had floated it to town, and upon dragging it out from the levee, had neglected to pour the water from the interior."

SECOND CALIFORNIA TOUR

Henri Herz returned to San Francisco in March of 1854 and gave three concerts, beginning April 2nd, and concluding with the fourth as a farewell engagement April 27th. Again he spent a short time in the interior, and returned with plans for a gala recital in June. On his way to the theatre he heard the cry of "fire." The flames made good progress. The theatre was consumed and with it Henri Herz's piano. While the flames devoured three-fourths of the town, the masons, architects and business men, instead of attempting to stop the destruction, entered into engagements to rebuild the city. Nothing could exceed the coolness of the Americans at this crisis; in many gambling houses, while the first floor was being reduced to ashes, they were trumping and turning up kings on the third. So, in a blaze of glory, figuratively speaking, Henri Herz bade farewell to San Francisco.

His experiences in California had been annoying, but they were at least exciting and profitable. Herz went to Mexico and on to the West Indies, his pockets filled with golden coins. He returned later to Paris where he lived a life of comparative luxury in more civilized surroundings.

SLUMBER SONG

In Paris one of his dreams was realized when his piano factory was established. The Conservatoire, where he had once been a pupil, added the name of Henri Herz to its faculty list. His piano compositions include eight concertos and over two hundred smaller works. All have been forgotten today with the exception of his Slumber Song, which has now been revised and issued as a theme melody for a radio program, and his still popular book of piano scales and exercises.

The works of Henri Herz, though brilliant, were merely studies in variations. They lacked the substance of the great masters or the melody of lesser composers. This may be attributed to some extent to his attitude toward the Parisians, whom he felt could appreciate only light, colorful music.

As an artist his brilliancy and bravura were immense, but he was lacking in the sturdier qualities. He knew what the public wanted, and he was able to give it to them. Herz was an excellent show-man. He possessed the rare gift essential in the theatre of personality. From the moment he stepped out of the wings, the audience felt the importance of the artist rather than the compositions or the method used in execution.

He loved flattery and recognition and often condemned the Californians for their lack of appreciation. With California gold he was able to return to a more sympathetic understanding among his friends in Paris. The chore of earning his daily bread was no longer important, and with security came contentment.

In 1888, at the age of 82, Herz died in Paris where he had lived most of his life, 'a Viennese in voluntary exile,' as he himself expressed it.

MISKA HAUSER (1822 - 1887)

Miska Hauser, christened Michael Hauser, was born in Pressburg, Hungary in 1822. His father, a dilettante violinist, had been closely associated with Ludwig Von Beethoven.

The child had inherited an aptitude for music and his toys were soon discarded in favor of a toy violin which he attempted to play. Conductor Konradin Kreutzer was quick to sense that within this child lay the hidden talent of a great violinist. He urged the father to give the boy training.

When young Michael was but twelve years of age he gave a performance in the local theatre where he won a most enthusiastic ovation. On this occasion Professor Boehm of the Conservatory of Vienna presented the boy with a new violin. The kindly professor saw to it that the Imperial and Royal Joseph Mayseder hear the boy play, and persuaded the famed artist to take Michael as a pupil.

In 1840 Michael's father accompanied him on a supposedly short concert tour which was successful, and brought him engagements for eight consecutive years in Germany, Denmark, Sweden, Norway, Finland and all of Russia to the Siberian frontier.

In 1848, when Michael returned to Vienna, he found that the songs of the beautiful blue Danube and the waltzes of Strauss drowned by the din of revolution. Back home in Pressburg, he devoted his time to study, composing and preparing for a tour through France and England.

He arrived in London in the latter months of 1849, but already his thoughts had turned to a new field to conquer. Miska Hauser decided to come to America to make a fortune.

BARNUM WAS RIGHT

The young artist was in for a sad disappointment regarding his compensation. His agent was the master showman P. T. Barnum who furnished Miska with many engagements, all the glory, but little money.

In 1852 Miska Hauser returned to New York and another tour, traveling by boat along the Ohio and Mississippi to the deep South and on to the magic of Havana with its tropic beauty of flowers and blossoms. About this time Hauser was brought to the realization that in the phrase "there's a fool born every minute" Barnum must have had him in mind.

FIDDLE FOR GOLD

Miska Hauser had two distinct reasons for his journey to California. The first and most important was to reap a golden harvest from the strings of his violin; secondly, to shake the dust of Barnum and all eastern agents from his feet. In Philadelphia he engaged the pianist Laveneau as his accompanist.

He sailed on the **Baltic** and after twelve days docked in San Juan de Morte. The passengers and their belongings were transferred to smaller boats, continued their journey across the isthmus, and arrived January 14, 1853. In recording the trip Hauser states:

> "Horses and mules were awaiting us, a thousand mules to carry baggage and merchandise across the Panama Isthmus--for a great price, of course, since the more passengers, the higher the fee. For each pound of load one dollar. My violin, which like a wife one should always keep an eye on, I took with me on a horse; a little box on each side and a third one on top. To avoid any ribbing or sarcasm from other people, I rode in front and kept my place all the way to Granada--it was a hard and sour ride of twelve miles, more so since I never before rode a horse. During this unforgettable tour and torture, any old place would have seemed to be a Moorish Palace to me. But what a surprise in Granada: a real and magnificent hotel, an Alhambra, with all its magic--and up-to-date; from its windows, for the first time in my life, I viewed the blue Pacific--an unforgettable and magnificent moment. I felt as if I had seen Heaven and stood at the Portals of Eternity."

After a few days of rest they boarded the steamer **Brother Jonathan** then considered the last word in luxury, where Miska Hauser was wined, dined and feasted in the style becoming to a gentleman and artist. He gave a benefit concert for the crew which netted three hundred dollars and was over-joyed when the captain asked for his portrait and with grand ceremony hung it in the social study.

SAN FRANCISCO

Majestically, the Brother Jonathan sailed into the harbor and docked at San Francisco, February 2, 1853. Hauser wrote home:

> "My arrival was a happy one, some of my friends from the United States expected me and many others yet unknown to me but I had been recom-mended. I was led to the hotel where the same Miss Catherine Hayes, the singer stayed..."

Hauser had played in concert with Miss Hayes in Christiania and New York. He found that Catherine Hayes had made a half million dollars in one short year in California. Prices here ranged from three to ten dollars per seat, where in Vienna people would complain about three florin. San Francisco was over-flowing with concert performers who had come to California to get rich. Halls and theatres were en-gaged and tickets sold weeks ahead of schedule. There were no troublesome agents with rash promises and greedy hands. Miska Hauser gave his first concert in San Francisco on Feb-ruary 9, 1853 at San Francisco Hall. Seats were five dollars top.

In his memoirs, he gives a vivid picture of San Francisco of the early fifties. It reads in part:

> "All in all, how glad I would be had I already turned my back on this America. But the magic

force of gold is holding me here in California. Selfishness is our goddess here; no means are too low nor too disreputable as long as it serves the purpose...Murder and manslaughter are everyday affairs and he who intends to stay any length of time in this much appraised El Dorado may better view the nightly sky and stars from the window of his 'Chambre Garni' from whatever nasty hotel he stays...I have been accepted with special excellence, as I am the friend of the first nobility in this city. Only four weeks here and have given my sixth concert. The expenses supercede my greatest expectations. Daily invitations and yet thirty dollars is the average daily expense. For washing a shirt one pays a laundress fifty cents. So much gold I have seen here, it almost blinded me and anybody who does not mine for gold, will try to get rich by ways of other adventurous speculations ...Poets, people with imagination, artists and men of the pen will find a healthier atmosphere in any old attic on the continent than here where all dreams of human virtue and greatness are dissolved with the dust of gold." 1

During his first winter Hauser attended the opera Martha. The production was so inferior that the artist could sit through but one act. His sympathy was with the composer whom, he remarked, would "have turned in his grave." He attended a Chinese playhouse and reveled in the gaudy costumes without understanding the play or the language. He met Count Mortis Rousselt de Boulbon, who had led an invasion into Mexico, but had been defeated. He described the count as a fearless adventurer in the truest sense of the word, who was also a highly intelligent and educated man of great importance in the community. The count was an excellent pianist, and Miska considering the Frenchman's popularity and his

---

1 Hauser, Miska. Aus dem Wanderbuche Eines Oesterreichischen Virtuosen (Leipzig: Herbig Verlag, 1859.)

ability to bring cash to the box office, engaged him for the next concert.

Miska Hauser soon discovered that Californians wanted variety and spice. They came to see the artist as well as hear him perform. A musician who was merely a musician, regardless of his ability, received a cool reception if he were unable to sell himself to the audience. Hauser attributed his success in California not to the fact that he was an artist but to his ability to please the public at the expense of his art. His popularity was immense during his entire sojourn in California.

In his letters Hauser relates how he formed a string quartet from the gambling houses which would have done honor to any European city. With this group he gave his farewell concert May 15, 1853, which was his twenty-sixth during his three months stay in San Francisco. This affair brought him over two thousand dollars, and lasted four hours due to the overwhelming requests for encores. The orchestra performed Beethoven's Lenore Overture and others. He relates that after a number, based on an Oriental melody, The Chinese in the audience became so enthusiastic that he was forced to hide in one corner of the theatre in order to survive the Chinese triumph.

MONTEZ BOOED: HAUSER HEROIC

Public tolerence had been tried to the limit regarding Montez. On her initial performance she was booed and hissed until she was finally forced to leave the stage amid a barrage of decayed eggs and apples. The theatre manager in order to prevent his theatre from being completely demolished, persuaded Hauser, for a consideration of six hundred dollars, to come forth with his violin to quiet the crowd. The artist faced the belligerant audience armed only with his bow and violin and with the soft strains of his magic instrument the audience was soon appeased.

His popularity was now at its peak. Banquets, receptions and balls were given in his honor. Even the Chinese sent a deputation to invite him to their section of the city. The newly formed quartette was a huge success. Hauser calls this group the mental quartette of equally attuned souls. All was progressing with smooth alacrity when the viola player, suffering from acute indigestion, died. Hauser states that "all the members of the orchestra had given recommendable examples, except one, a Bohemian contra bass player, who expected compensation for his work."

HERE AND THERE

In his memoirs Hauser mentions many interesting situations in which he found himself. A gambling den where one paid for admission on leaving; a Chinese funeral resembling a Halloween party that began with a parade and ended in a display of fireworks; a duel between a newspaper editor named Swift and a Doctor Wolfe, the latter being killed while the object of their affections looked on from the balcony.

Possibly the most amusing incident was regarding a barber shop which bore his illustrious name. It seems that near the shop some California sign painter made a cartoon of the artist, picturing him with a long black beard and holding his violin in an ingracious manner. Hauser offered the artist forty dollars to remove the picture, but the request was ignored. At last, in order to save his reputation, he settled for one hundred dollars.

In Stockton the artist was required to give an exhibition of courage during one of his concerts. Suddenly the audience arose and cried in fear, for the door to the adjoining hall had been pushed down by the immense crowd and revealed a full grown tiger. The tiger was in a cage, but the audience was too overwrought to see this. Quiet was restored and the unwelcome guest remained throughout the concert.

FAREWELL

After ten months in San Francisco, the artist toured through South America and eventually returned to San Francisco where he remained for a long period of time. While in Panama he paid a visit to Ole Bull who was stricken with fever. Ole Bull informed him that Schubert the publisher had already printed Hauser's composition Bird in the Tree. The publication of this number was to have been withheld until Hauser returned to Europe.

Eventually Miska Hauser did return to Europe where he lived on the fruits of his American adventure. He retired to Vienna where he purchased a large estate, and remained in seclusion save for an occasional concert. He died December 8, 1887.

OLE BORNEMANN BULL (1810 - 1880)

Ole Bornemann Bull was born in Bergen, Norway in 1810. His father, a physician, was opposed to a musical career and sent Ole to the University of Christiania to study theology. The boy soon found a place as a conductor of a musical and dramatic society in the city. Ole Bull was eventually dismissed from the University for agitation and conduct unbecoming to a gentleman, following a public demonstration. Spohr, the distinguished violinist of the period, had always been Ole Bull's idol and from the artist he hoped to gain sympathetic understanding. The artist granted the young aspirant an audience, but gave him a cool reception. His spirits dampened, he journeyed to Gottingen where his boisterous conduct involved him in a duel; he was requested to leave the country.

Ole Bull had studied violin with Paulsen and later Bundbolim. In the main, however, he was a self-taught player. His individuality was so strongly marked as to leave but little room for the direct influence of a teacher.

After successful concerts in Norway he went to Paris, but was refused admittance to the Conservatorie. In Paris he heard Paganini whose playing made an immense impression on him. He threw himself with the utmost vigor into the pursuit of technical studies in order to emulate the feats performed by the Italian virtuoso. The result was a complete breakdown. After his recovery he played in Paris and started for Italy where he created a perfect furore. In sixteen months Bull played two hundred and seventy-four concerts throughout England, Scotland and Ireland.

OLE BULL: INDIVIDUALIST

Accompanied by much fan fare, pomp and ceremony, Ole Bull came to America in 1853. Critics found him a man of remarkable character and an artist of undoubted genius. They found his execution technically perfect, but his interpretation was lost in mechanical efficiency. Musicians called him a trickster because he used an almost flat bridge in his violin which enabled him to produce beautiful effects by playing chords and passages in form parts. He appeared to have been conscious of his inability to do justice to serious music so, with exception of one or two movements of Paganini, he played his own compositions. His private rendering of quartettes is said to have proved his wisdom of self-restraint. Musicians raised cultured eyebrows when Ole Bull played, but audiences thronged to hear him and were carried away by his brilliance.

CALIFORNIA TOUR

Ole Bull arrived in San Francisco July 15, 1854 accompanied by Maurice Strakosch, pianist. His first concertat the Metropolitan Theatre was extremely successful from a box office standpoint but failed to live up to the expectations of the critics. They labeled Ole Bull as the novelty of the month.

In San Francisco Ole Bull met many of his old friends and admirers. They were gathered here from many lands where they had listened to his magic tones before in far distant homes. His reception then, was a pleasant one that must have surpassed the fondest hope of a man who had excited everywhere an enthusiasm unparalleled in the history of instrumental triumph. However, the trickster legend had followed him to California. Regarding his introductory concert, one critic wrote in The Pioneer of August 18, 1854:

> "Ole Bull's power is now wanting. We believe
> that it only sleeps, or that perhaps he does
> not appreciate a California audience. Tricks
> upon the violin we have witnessed usque ad
> nauseam. They are the accomplishments of the
> juggler. Does Ole Bull consider us incapable
> of appreciating genius? Let him appeal to the
> heart of his audience--not to the fancy. We
> have heard that he has suffered from ill health
> --that he is enfeebled by sickness--that in
> fact Ole Bull is not himself. This must be the
> cause, for his heart was not in his work. He
> played skillfully, but mechanically. The se-
> lections of music too, were not judicious. Is
> there nothing new under the sun? Must we ever
> hear the 'Carnival of Venice?' and poor 'Yankee
> Doodle'--no great affair at its best, and very
> difficult to make music of--must our ears for-
> ever be tortured with distortions of this mis-
> erable air? Away with these abominations--this
> wretched trickery..."

Ole Bull followed with concerts on July 26 and August 5, 1854. He made a short trip into the interior, returning August 26. Four concerts followed one of which was a benefit for Mrs. Catherine Sinclair, an actress and former wife of Forrest, who was at the time acting manager at the Metropolitan Theatre in San Francisco. His farewell concert was held September 14, followed by a hasty departure for New York. He was scheduled to return to San Francisco in 1870.

DECLARATION OF INDEPENDENCE

With his return to New York, Bull attempted to man-
age an opera company and took over the Academy of Music. He
offered a prize of $1,000 for the best original opera by an
American composer on a strictly American subject. In his
announcement he gave native composers a chance to declare
their independence. However, the Academy closed its doors in
March 1855 and the venture perished.

A SCANDINAVIAN UTOPIA

It took more than the failure of an opera company
to daunt Ole Bull. His new plan was to establish a colony in
Pennsylvania called "Olena" where he would found a new Norway, consecrated to freedom, and protected by the mighty flag
of the Union.

His Utopia like most of his plans, never became a
reality. Ole Bull found himself a victim of frauds who had
no legal title to the land. After an expensive law suit, he
returned to Europe, where he remained for ten years in comparative retirement.

ROBERT NICOLAS BOCHSA (1789 - 1856)

Robert Nicolas Bochsa was born in Montmedy, France,
August 9, 1789. According to the law then existing in France
his birth was illegitimate. His father was Karl Bochsa, a
flute and clarinet player, who died in 1821. One of his bio-
graphers seems to believe that Bochsa's birth and early life
might have had some bearing on his character as a man.

Before he was sixteen, his opera <u>Trajan</u> was produced at Lyons in honor of the Emperor. In Bordeaux he became a pupil of Franz Beck, wrote a ballet, and an oratorio <u>Le Déluge Universal</u>. In 1806 he entered the Conservatorie at Paris where he studied the harp with Madermann and Marin. Soon however, he formed a style of his own. Bochsa was continually discovering new effects and is said to have completely revolutionized the method of harp playing. In 1813 he **was** appointed harpist to the Emperor Napoleon, three years later to Louis XVIII. He composed a requiem to the memory of Louis XVI which was performed with great solemnity in 1816. A year later he was detected in extensive forgeries and **fled** from France, never to return. Bochsa was tried in his absence and condemned to twelve years imprisonment, with a fine of four thousand francs.

SVENGALI AND TRILBY

Bochsa took refuge in London where his infrequent concerts were met with enthusiasm, but his forte seemed to be that of an instructor rather than as a performer. Many believed that Bochsa was endowed with hypnotic power. A London critic reviewing the recital of one of Bochsa's pupils remarked:

> "His pupils play as though inspired by some unseen spirit. Strange that their ability to execute disappears with the master's presence."

While in London the harpist became involved with the wife of Sir Henry Bishop. Under Bochsa's influence Anna

Bishop became a renowned star of both opera and concert. Whether this influence was due to legendary hypnotic power or prompted by infatuation on the singer's part is a matter of opinion. After a short time Madam Bishop eloped with Bochsa and created an international scandal. After a short tour of Europe Madam Bishop and Bochsa came to America. At this time the harpist was basking in reflected glory from Madam Bishop. The two souls seem to have found each other without the benefit of clergy; upon this affair De Maurier is said to have written his famous classic Trilby.

In the East, Bishop and Bochsa received only a mild reception as artists and were socially ignored. In 1841 Sir Henry Bishop died.

Bochsa and Madam Bishop arrived in San Francisco February 2, 1854 where the singer was heralded as a star of the first magnitude. Bochsa remained in the background with the exception of infrequent professional appearances, then only in joint concerts with Madam Bishop. In September 1855 Madam Bishop performed Bochsa's Voyage Musicale.

THE SPELL IS BROKEN

Due to failing health Bochsa, accompanied by Madam Bishop, sailed for Australia September 30, 1855 arriving December 3. A month after their arrival in Sydney, January 7, 1856, Bochsa passed away. The spell was broken, but Trilby sang on. Many critics of the time said that while her voice remained powerful and technically perfect, the fire was gone.

In spite of her marriage to Martin Schultz she   remained   a
faithful friend to Bochsa, for during the remainder   of   her
life she made repeated visits to his tomb.

Other visiting celebrities of the era   (1849-1865)
included: singers John W. Connor, Josephine D'Orme, Rosalie
Durand,   Mme. Drusilla Garbato,   Mrs. M. G. Goodenow, Anna
Griswald, Stephen Massett, Herr Mengis, Hans Orlic, Carlotta
Patti, Henrietta Sontag, Anna Thillon, Annie Urie, Mme. Von
Gulpen, Minnie Walton; pianists Mons. Charles Chenal, George
T. Evans, Louis Gottschalk, Charles Schultz, Maurice   Strak-
osch, Josephine Van der Broeck, Von Imloff, Rod Sipp;   vio-
linists John Kelly, Martin Simonson, Charles Staderman,Chas.
Thillon; and conductors George T. Evans,   Signor   Garbato,
Fred Lyster and William Saurin.

GRAND CONCERT,

MUSICAL HALL,

FRIDAY EVENING, OCTOBER 8th, 1858.

— ♦ —

Mr. & Mrs. LEACH beg to announce that their next Concert will take place at the above Hall, on Friday Evening, October 8th, 1858.

The following artists will appear:

Mrs. GEORGIANA STUART LEACH,

Miss ANNA GRISWOLD,

Mr. HEROLD,	Mr. G. A. SCOTT,
Mr. McKORKELL,	SIG. FERRER,
Mr. ELLIOT,	Mr. LEACH.

Mr. HEROLD will preside at the Piano Forte.

— ♦ —

TICKETS, ... 50 CENTS EACH,

May be obtained, with Programmes, at Atwill's, Lecount's and Woodworth's, and at the door on the evening of the Concert.

Seats may be secured on the day of the Concert at the Hall, from 10 o'clock, A. M., until 2 o'clock, P. M.

Concert to commence at 8 o'clock.

Towne & Bacon, Printers, 125 Clay Street.

CHAPTER TWELVE: <u>LOCAL PERSONAGES</u>

ot all the musicians who came cared to re-
turn to countries that had grown   weary
with the weight of centuries. Soon they
found that San Francisco was the   promised land for which they had been seeking. Here they would build their castles
and reap a still greater harvest.

<u>CHRISTIAN KOPPITZ</u> (1829 - 1861)

Christian Koppitz was born in Hamburg, Germany in
1829. He was a musical genius not only as a performer, but
as a composer. Through the medium of his magic flute, Koppitz achieved world-wide distinction. He had inherited an
aptitude for music from both parents who were musicians of
some note. The boy began his studies in Hamburg, going later
to Bremen where he became an outstanding performer with an
orchestra.

At an early age Christian Koppitz had played throughout Europe to audiences who were spellbound by his brilliance
of tone, and were astounded by the fact that Koppitz was able
to produce sequences of double notes in two-part harmony.
Such a feat heretofore had been considered impossible.

In 1849, accompanied by his brother Henri, he made his first visit to America. His fame as a performer spread throughout the East. Some critics even went so far as to say that he played on a "magic flute" equipped with some mechanical device in order to perform the two-part harmony. After many successful engagements the brothers turned their thoughts westward, arriving in San Francisco in 1853. Koppitz made his first professional appearance on April 13th of that year.

The founding of the Germania Concert Society, of which Christian Koppitz became a prominent figure, was an important step in the history of San Francisco music. The purpose of the organization, as stated by the San Francisco Chronicle of February 13, 1856, was "to popularize music, especially music of the highest order, to educate the people, to soften their manners and wean their minds from low sensual pleasures, and to direct them to that which sympathizes with and is akin to good." The orchestra numbered about thirty musicians and was directed by Rudolph Herold.

During the second subscription concert of the society, Christian Koppitz and J. Froehling performed a "Duo Concertante" for two flutes for the first time in California. It might be interesting to note the much criticised program which appeared in the San Francisco Chronicle of February 28, 1856, and the reviewer's comments on the following day:

PROGRAMME

```
1 Overture to Martha.....................Flotow
2 The Artists' Pilgrimage Waltz........Labitzky
3 Cavatina from
     Lucia di Lammermoor...............Donizetti
                Signora Garbato
```

4 Introduction and Variations Brilliante, on a
   theme from Semiramide for Two Flutes
         C. Koppitz and J. Froehling
5 Adagio and Finale from L. Von Beethoven's
   Grand Symphonie in C Minor
6 Overture to William Tell.............Rossini
7 Grand Scene and Romance from   the   opera
   Ernani (written originally for Baritone)
   sung for the first time by Signora Garbato.
8 Helen Polka
9 Canzone Veneziana, composed by Garbato.

"The second subscription concert of the Germania
Concert Society took place last night in the
Music Hall.   The pieces in the programme are
very beautiful, but it must be said that some
of them appeared to be considered very tedious
by the greater number of the audience. The
Adagio, Scherzo and Finale of Beethoven's Symphonie in C Minor, for instance, are portions
of a very grand and celebrated composition, yet
they caused many to yawn.

"Then to add to the heaviness of the entertainment the vocal music was given in a foreign
tongue...Then the vexed and exhausted hearer
thinks how more agreeable would be some plain
old song, in his own vernacular, to all those
foreign unintelligible doremifas. The Germania
Concert Society would do well to consider this
matter. The classical character of their concerts may best delight themselves and the con-
noisseur in music; yet they play music not for
the few but for many....Mme. Garbato's singing
did not strike us as being particularly effective."

Christian Koppitz lived in San Francisco from 1853
until the spring of 1859, when he made a trip to Europe where
his professional reputation was already established.   In June
1859, while visiting England, he had the honor of performing
before Her Majesty Queen Victoria, and for several Philharmonic concerts. Speaking of him on that occasion the London
News states in part:

"He performs his own music which independently
of its unheard of difficulties, has much originality, beauty and expression.   Whether his

peculiar methods of producing effects can be taught to others, we know not, but if they can, Mr. Koppitz may be the founder of a new school of flute playing, which will enhance the influence and importance of this elegant instrument."

Koppitz was the heart and soul of San Francisco musical societies, and among other accomplishments is remembered for his rendition of the Nightingale Polka at Maguire's Opera House. The Daily Alta California on February 17, 1861 wrote:

"In an orchestra he was invaluable, and no vocalist who once was accompanied by him, was willing to sing to others on the flute. He accompanied nearly every vocalist of note who visited California up to 1850."

Christian Koppitz died in Havana where he was engaged as director for an Italian Opera Company. He had crowded into thirty-two years a lifetime of brilliance and artistry.

RUDOLPH HEROLD (1832 - 1889)

Finding his son, Rudolph, strongly and passionately attached to music as a study, to the exclusion of law, medicine, or theology, Rev. Herold resolved to settle this foolish whim once and for all and dissuade his son against the path of life he wished to adopt. The pious and learned man felt that the public life of a musician was unbecoming to the dignity of a minister's son. Unable to convince Rudolph himself, he wrote to his friend Felix Mendelssohn whose very presence should have been enough to frighten the boy. In due time Mendelssohn replied:

Rev. Herold
Bibra, Germany

My dear Sir: I shall take a great pleasure in
assisting you in the serious and important matter which you have written me to the best of my
knowledge and ability. At the end of this month
you will not find me any more in Leipzig. If
you could possibly arrange to meet me here before my departure on the 8th instant, we will
and must find time to talk over the future of
your son, on which occasion it would be desir-
able for me to make the personal acquaintance
of the young gentleman, if I am to render any
decision. With sincere respect, I remain yours
truly

Felix Mendelssohn Bartholdy

Bibra, a small German village, where Rudolph Herold

was born March 29, 1832, was but sixteen miles from Leipzig,

the important musical center of the district. Rudolph was

sixteen at the time, and to test his skill as a musician the

great master asked him to play a very difficult piano number

on sight. His rendition of the selection was the turning

point of Rudolph's life. The result of the interview with

Mendelssohn was that the father put away his pride and sacri-

ficed his own selfish hopes. He realized that the boy was a

potential artist.

In 1847 young Rudolph entered the Conservatory of

Leipzig where he worked with Moscheles, Rietz and Hauptmann.

He became associated with a prominent musical organization

attached to the Cathedral and was appointed "Chor Perfect."

He was graduated from the Conservatory in 1851 and in the same

year left his home to come to America.

Rudolph Herold's first American appearance was as accompanist for Emma Gillingham Bostwick. Critics were quick to compare his execution and manner to that of Thalberg and other pianists of the period. He was engaged to assist Miss Catherine Hayes, singer, and accompanied her to California, arriving in San Francisco in 1852.

After Catherine Hayes' departure Rudolph Herold made San Francisco his American home, and here he remained, with but few intermissions, until his death.

In a short time Herold became an important figure in San Francisco society, with his finger in every musical pie. He gave lessons, conducted musical societies both English and German, directed Italian operas, and was chorus director for the Philharmonic Society founded in 1854 by himself and Signor Robert Bochsa. In addition to his many activities, social and professional, Rudolph Herold acted as organist for both St. Mary's Cathedral and the First Unitarian church for a period of twenty years.

By 1870 Rudolph Herold had reached the peak of his popularity. He had appeared in concert with Catherine Hayes, Miska Hauser, Koppitz, as well as concerts where he was the featured artist. He had conducted all the better known choral groups of the city. The San Francisco News Letter under date of August 28, 1875, remarks:

> "Platt's Hall. Professor Herold's après midi
> concerts have become so extremely popular that
> an immense and fashionable audience filled the
> house on Wednesday afternoon. Music has become
> a necessity to our pleasure loving people, and
> musicians have certainly recognized the fact.
> Furthermore, the class of music given at these
> après midis is of so high an order as to set
> the seal of fashion upon them, and to redeem
> them from the odium which by some means became
> attached to matinees."

The San Francisco Bulletin, April 5, 1858 is quoted:

> "Grand Concert This Evening. The grand concert
> for the benefit of the Church of the Advent will
> take place at Musical Hall this evening. It
> will be under the conduct of Rudolph Herold.
> The programme comprises choice collections from
> operas and oratorios. The 'Wedding March,' from
> Midsummer Nights Dream, a selection from Mozart's
> Don Juan, the overture to Der Windschutz, and
> other fine pieces will be given."

From the San Francisco News Letter we learn that on October 9,
1875:

> "Herold's Concerts at Platt's Hall have proved a
> success in every way. They are certainly the
> best orchestral concerts we have ever had on
> this coast."

Rudolph Herold made two trips abroad during his residence in San Francisco. Upon his return, in 1874, he suf-
fered a long illness followed by a slight stroke of paralysis.
After his recovery he organized an orchestra of fifty-two
pieces, but his capacity for work, due to ill health, was by
this time on the wane. It is impossible to enumerate the many
contributions Rudolph Herold made to music in San Francisco.
He introduced to the music loving people artists whom they
could not have otherwise enjoyed except by visiting the European centers of music or the eastern states. He was now living on his reputation, a position well earned. His orchestra

appeared in concert with varied response. From The Argonaut
of October 26, 1878, the following paragraph is quoted:

"In view of the fact that Mr. Herold's orchestra was this week compelled to forego one of
its usual rehearsals, and this added fact that
it never seems to have quite enough of them at
the best (and that consequently, the loss of one
is really a very serious matter) it would be
scarcely fair to deal with the performance at
last Wednesday's matinee from any severly critical standpoint. In such cases the conductor-
himself, at least, quite as sensitive to all
shortcomings as the most exacting audiences--
is entitled to sympathy; and, if, under such
circumstances, we get anything like a reason-
ably smooth performance, one without mishaps or
serious blemishes, I, for one, am ready to be
easily satisfied, with nothing but gratitude to
the giver of the feast, and a hope that all may
go better next time. I wish it were also pos-
sible to look forward to better programmes in
the future; programmes in which the search for
novelties might carry Mr. Herold's experience
of repertory backward to an occasional recollec-
tion of the fact that Mozart and Haydn also composed symphonies that will still bear listening
to; in which there should be recognizable a
somewhat more logical (I won't say aesthetic,
although that's what I mean) arrangement of the
various numbers, or in which one might occasionally get through an afternoon without four
horns, four trumpets, (cornet-a-piston) and
three trombones, not to mention side drums and
triangle."

Rudolph Herold remained active in music circles until about 1886 when ill health forced his retirement from public life. He passed away July 25, 1880 a victim of paralysis.

Recognizing the dramatic possibilities of Rudolph
Herold's life, Columbia Pictures Corporation are at present
(1939) preparing a feature production based on the life of
San Francisco's adopted son.

STEPHEN W. LEACH

Stephen W. Leach, one of the important figures **of** San Francisco's musical history was born in London, England. He made his debut as a Shakespearean actor at the Drury Lane Theatre, in London, where Sir Henry Bishop was musical director. The English public found Leach a versatile actor, but completely lacking in the culture and grace required of a public idol. He came to New York where he joined a Shakespearean repertoire company and toured through the eastern states, meeting with only a mild reception. Fortunately, Stephen Leach was endowed with a fine singing voice as well as with a knowledge of music. In New York he met Madam Anna Thillon, and with her light-opera troupe came to San Francisco.

Mr. Leach made his first professional appearance January 13, 1854 with Julia Gould, Miss Marie Leach, L. T. Zander and I. C. Smith. This group, known as The Mountaineers, dedicated themselves to folk music and "homey" songs. On January 16, Stephen Leach appeared in a song and Shakespearean recital. In May 1854 Madam Anna Thillon's Opera Company presented <u>Cinderella</u> with the following cast:

```
"Cinderella....................Mme. Anna Thillon
Fairy Queen...................Miss Julia Gould
Clorinda......................Miss Julia Pelby
Felix.........................Mr. Hudson (sic)
Baron Pompolino...............Herr Mengis
Dandine.......................Mr. Stephen Leach
     N. B. Children in arms not admitted."
```

Stephen Leach made his debut as a director on June 21, 1854 with the Sängerbund and Philharmonic Societies presenting David's <u>Le Désert</u>. This concert was repeated on June

28 and July 7. He made a trip to the east in 1855, returning to San Francisco with Mrs. Leach on March 31, 1858. As Bret Harte's brother-in-law, (he had married the poet's sister) his social status had taken on a new importance. He was a member of both the California Theatre and the Baldwin Stock Companies. On June 3, 1858 he appeared with Mrs. Leach in a joint concert. Quoting from the Wide West of June 6, 1858:

> "The first concert of Mr. Stephen Leach, Mrs. Georgina Stuart Leach and Miss Anna Griswald, took place at the Musical Hall on Thursday night. It occured unfortunately that Mrs. Leach could not appear, being unprepared for the contingency, arranged that the concert should proceed, but declined to receive any tickets that had been purchased; informing all who came that the same tickets would likewise admit them to the next concert...Mr. Leach's honest manly voice was heard again with real pleasure, and his reception evinced the high appreciation he justly holds with our music loving community. Rudolph Herold ably assisted in the instrumental department, and the evening's entertainment afforded a degree of enjoyment that has not been experienced by the lovers of music for many, many months."

During the next few years San Francisco grew to love Stephen Leach. His principal interest seemed to be in choral societies where he developed many interesting groups. In 1893 he returned to the legitimate theatre to play in As You Like It, and although the critics were kind, they found Stephen Leach's method of acting antiquated. Even his efforts as choral director were on the wane.

Stephen Leach became librarian for the Bohemian Club where he directed the choral music for their many entertainments. The obstacle was that the club's by-laws forbade any member occupying a paid position in the club or receiving of any remuneration from that body. In order to overcome this difficulty, Uncle Stephen, as he was affection- ately known, was requested to resign in order to obtain the position. The actor refused to submit himself to such a hu- miliation but was finally persuaded to tender his resignation. Jerome Hart speaking of the incident in his book, <u>In Our Sec- ond Century</u>, page 343, recalls a humorous situation:

> "One day I entered the library, and observed Uncle Stephen at his task; he was seated at a table heaped with books; before him was a large blank book for cataloguing; a pen was in his fingers, but he was sound asleep. Behind him stood Harry Brady, shaking with silent mirth. I asked him the cause and Brady whispered: 'He is indexing Shakespeare under T.' 'Where does he get the T From?' I queried, wonderingly. 'From the word THE,' replied Brady, 'he is in- dexing it as The Works of Shakespeare.' Our chuckling aroused Uncle Stephen, who awoke with a start and fell to writing vigorously."

Stephen Leach did a great service to San Francisco by assisting to place its infant feet in the path-way toward music. He was one of those individuals who never quite ar- rive. His acting was tolerable but never brilliant; his sing- ing pleasant but never masterful. He was always a featured player, never the star. As a director and teacher he found his forte. San Francisco owes a debt of gratitude to Stephen W. Leach.

GEORGE LODER (1816 - 1867)

George Loder was born in Bath, England in 1816. He studied pianoforte and organ, but his talent seemed bent toward an ability to conduct rather than execute. Europe turned a deaf ear to Loder's work as an artist, but it acclaimed him as a composer. By the time he had reached his twenty-fifth year, he had to his credit several symphonies and four operas, all of which had been successfully performed in London. In 1845 he came to New York where critics listened to his playing, but failed to respond.

Loder arrived in San Francisco February 26, 1852. His first professional work was that of director for a series of five concerts given by Signora Biscaccianti and the celebrated pianist-composer George T. Evans who was acting as Mme. Biscaccianti's accompanist.

George Loder attempted several concerts in San Francisco, first as a pianist and later as an organist. He was soon to discover that in the West people were of practically the same opinion as the audiences of New York and Europe. As a director and conductor he was applauded by press and speech, but when he played, the public, out of respect to the artist, merely listened. Regarding one of his many orchestral concerts a critic remarks:

> "As has been mentioned elsewhere it was thought that the orchestra was weak and feeble. Mr. Loder attempts to remedy this defect with his piano; but that is an utter abomination. The remarks made were that the piano is essentially

a solo instrument and does not harmonize well
with many instruments. Loder belongs on the
conductor's stand, baton in hand, directing in
forces. When he is in his proper place the audience will be completely satisfied."

After years of study to perfect his art, George Loder was forced to forsake the piano for the baton. Under his
guidance many famous stars made their bows to San Francisco,
among whom were Kate Hayes, Miska Hauser, and Ole Bull. Anna
Thillon presented her English opera, January 16, to February
10, 1854, under his direction.

George Loder, like Rudolph Herold, seemed to have
had his part in practically every musical activity. His name
appears with nearly every important musical event in San
Francisco between 1852 and 1856. One of the more important
of the musical societies was The Pacific Musical Troupe which
opened July 26, 1853. The San Francisco Daily Herald of the
preceeding day is quoted as follows:

> "The new Musical Hall on Bush Street will be
> opened tomorrow night, on which occasion The
> Pacific Musical Troupe, supported by a chorus
> consisting of the Philharmonic Society of this
> city, and a fine orchestra, will make their
> first appearance. The Troupe consists of Mrs.
> Leach, contralto; Mr. J. Beutler, tenor, and
> Mr. J. C. Smith, basso. We have had the pleas-
> ure of hearing them in rehearsal and we do not
> hesitate to predict for them a most favorable
> reception from the lovers of music in this city.
> They are all skillful and scientific musicians,
> and possessed of fine natural voices improved
> by cultivation. Mr. Beutler, as a tenor, will
> compare favorably with many of high reputation
> abroad...The Philharmonic Society includes a
> number of our best amateur singers, well dis-
> ciplined, under the management of Mr. Meiggs
> and Mr. George Loder. The latter gentleman of-
> ficiates as the director of these entertain-
> ments."

The Pacific Musical Troupe was an outstanding success and although scheduled for but three concerts, they were compelled to give five to capacity houses. On August 14, 1855, St. Mary's Cathedral dedicated a new organ and presented a sacred oratorio. The solo parts were sung by Madam Anna Bishop, Mme. Von Gulpen, and Messrs. White, Leglaise and Mengis. George Loder officiated at the console, while Rudolph Herold directed the chorus work of the Philharmonic Society.

By the year 1855 George Loder had reached the peak of his popularity. An operatic venture, however, soon proved to be his undoing. Loder had promised by verbal agreement, to produce a series of Italian operas to feature Signora Garbato who, in turn was to furnish the necessary funds. The opera was put into rehearsal, but several days before the opening, Loder refused to have anything more to do with the production. A damage suit followed in which the Signora charged fraud and libel as well as misrepresentation of funds.

Shortly after the hearing of this suit, George Loder left San Francisco for Australia. The Australians chose to ignore the unfavorable publicity Loder had recently received in America and presented him with a meerschaum pipe richly mounted with gold and in a silver case.

His life in Australia was a continuation of the activity and energy he had displayed in San Francisco. He died July 15, 1867 in Adelaide, South Australia. He was but fifty-one years of age at the time of his death but his life had been a profitable one both to himself and to his fellow man.

Many of the artists who came to San Francisco as visiting celebrities with the idea of filling their pockets with gold dust remained to transmit their respective professions to a younger generation. Among those of the first magnitude who stayed on as conductors or teachers or performing artists were Charles Schultz, W. McKorkell, David W. Loring, J. H. Dohrmann, Herr Kehler, George W. Williams, George Edmonds, Signor Pellegrini, John Froehling, Mme. Planel, Don Manuel Ferrar, Anna Griswald, E. Pique, Mons. and Mme. Pettinos and Louis Schmidt. The pedagogues included several composers such as Christian Koppitz, W. McKorkell, G. A. Scott, Signor Garbato, P. R. Nichols, L. T. Planel and Edward Rimbault whose compositions helped to establish a creative cultural tradition in San Francisco.

As stated in the prefatory note, the main object of this volume has been to unfold the Gold Rush decade's leading themes and to present from a hundred years' perspective the pattern which appears. Needless to say, each chapter of the book could well become the subject of a separate volume. However, if the work has given the reader a glimpse of a great western city's musical beginnings -- an epoch which embraces Indian singers of the Gregorian Chant, Spanish troubadours, and Barbary Coast ballad-mongers; minstrels, makers of accordions, choir-singers and world-renowned visiting virtuosi -- it has served its purpose.

THE END

MILESTONES IN EARLY MUSIC
(Chronological Summary)

1827 Four piece Indian orchestra at Mission Dolores, increased to fourteen pieces in year 1827.

1846 Andrew Hoeppner, first piano teacher, arrived in Sonoma County. General Vallejo and family were his pupils.

1849 Philadelphia Minstrels were first San Francisco minstrels, appearing at Bella Union, on October 22. Charles Rhodes, composer, first rendered "The Days of Old, The Days of Gold, and The Days of '49" at The Aguila de Oro Music Hall.

1850 First "Grand Concert" given Dec. 22, at California Exchange, Commercial and Clay Streets. Tom Maguire opened first Jenny Lind Theatre with a concert.

1850 Henri Herz, first concert pianist to visit San Francisco, March 26th.

1851 Arrival in San Francisco of Dr. Augustus H. Malech, father of San Francisco Choral Music.

1851 The Pellegrini Opera Company was the first important operatic troupe. About ninety different opera companies have visited the city since 1851.

1851 The first complete Grand Opera given in San Francisco was Bellini's La Sonnambula, performed at the Adelphi on February 12; Norma was produced on February 27; Ernani, on April 8.

1852 First oratorio in San Francisco, Rossini's Stabat Mater. Largest and best organ on Pacific Coast, in Calvary Presbyterian Church.

1852 The first concert was given at the Bella Union. Sale of seats for Kate Hayes Concert, given as a benefit for the Firemen's Charitable Fund. First choice bought by Sam Brannan for $500.

1852 The first grand opera season in San Francisco.

1852 After one of Kate Hayes' concerts, well known San Francisco men removed horses from the diva's carriage and themselves drew it to the hotel.

1852 The first song dedicated to a lady of San Francisco was titled 'Greeting to California', poem by Alfred Wheeler; music by George Loder.

1852 A Chinese Dramatic Company, the Tong Hook Tong Co., consisting of 123 performers accompanied by an orchestra of their own music, appeared at the American Theatre.

1852 Eliza Biscaccianti was the first great prima donna to come West. She appeared in San Francisco under P. T. Barnum's management.

1852 George Loder began as an orchestra leader in the American Theatre. Later he organized the first Philharmonic Society of San Francisco.

1852 Rudolph H. Herold, San Francisco's first choral director, arrived in San Francisco on November 20, as a piano accompanist of Catherine Hayes.

1852   San Francisco Philharmonic Society, first outstanding musical organization. Rudolph Herold, leading musician of the period, 1850-60.

1853   Miska Hauser, violinist, arrived in San Francisco. Played first concert February 9, 1853.

1853   Citizens of San Francisco presented Kate Hayes with a card case made of California gold.

1853   Four German Societies in San Francisco, devoted to music.

1854   February 2, arrival in San Francisco of Madame Anna Bishop and Robert Boscha, harpist.

1854   July 15, arrival in San Francisco of Ole Bull, Maurice Strakosch, and Adelina Patti.

1854   Turner Gesang Verein boasted 6000 members.

1854   A performance of Der Freischutz in German was given at the Metropolitan Theatre. "At the close of the second act the gas went out all over the theatre and the audience departed."

1854   Large music hall erected in Bush Street by Henry Meiggs, speculator. He was first president of San Francisco Philharmonic Society.

1854   On Dec. 23, the Turnverein Hall was dedicated in the presence of 2000 persons.

1855   First weekly concert by Germania concert Turnverein. A law forbidding on Sunday noisey and barbarous amusements went into effect.
First appearance of Carlotta Patti, as a vocalist, Union Theatre.
First promenade Concert by George Loder at Russ Gardens.

1855   First appearance Paul Julian, six year old violin prodigy, Music Hall.
First representation, oratorio, The Creation, at Musical Hall.

1856   First appearance Frances A. Blodgett, accordionist.

1856   The arrival of a large steamer was such important news as to empty churches or concert halls at a moment's notice.

1857   The First Annual German Festival in California began July 23, 1857. It lasted four days.

1858   The Lyceum inaugurated matinee minstrel performances, which were well patronized by women.
In the latter 50's and early 60's San Francisco became the minstrel show production center of the world.

1860   The three most popular operas during the first decade (1850-60) were La Fille du Regiment, Norma, and The Crown Diamonds.

VOLUME I: MUSIC OF THE GOLD RUSH ERA

A P P E N D I C E S

    A.   BARBARY COAST MUSIC HALLS

    B.   FIREMEN'S ORGANIZATIONS

    C.   CHURCHES AND CHURCH CHOIRS

    D.   CHORAL SOCIETIES

    E.   ORCHESTRAS

    F.   OPERA COMPANIES

    G.   MINSTREL TROUPES

    H.   MUSIC TEACHERS

    I.   VISITING CELEBRITIES

    J.   COMPOSERS AND WORKS

    K.   INSTRUMENT MAKERS

    L.   MUSIC DEALERS

    M.   MUSIC PUBLISHERS

APPENDIX A.

BARBARY COAST MUSIC HALLS: (Most prominent ones)

Aguila de Oro
Alhambra
Arcade
Bella Union
Bill Briggs'
Dennison's Exchange
El Dorado
Empire
Fontine House
La Sociedad
Mazourka
Parker House
Polka
St. Charles
Steve Whipple's
Varsouvienne
Verandah
Ward House

CHIEF HOTELS

1846 City Hotel, Clay Street and Montgomery Street.
1849 Saint Francis Hotel, Montgomery Street and California
        Street.
1850 Jones Hotel (later the Tehama House), Sansome Street
        and California Street.
1852 Oriental Hotel, Bush Street and Battery Street.
        Wilson's Exchange, Sansome Street near Sacramento Street.
1853 Rassette House, Bush Street and Sansome Street.
1854 International House, Jackson Street near Kearny Street.

POPULAR RESTAURANTS

Delmonico's
Franklin House
Irving House
Jackson House
Lafayette House
Sutter House
The Fountain Head
Winn's Branch

B. FIRE DEPARTMENTS OF SAN FRANCISCO *

*Firemen and Fire Departments
were the most prominent music
sponsors of early San Francisco.
(See Chapter IV).

Founded	Name	Location
April 14, 1850	Empire Co. No. 1	Kearny St. bet. Sacramento and California Sts.
June 15, 1850	Howard Co. No.3	Commercial St. bet. Sansome & Montgomery
June 15, 1850	Lady Washington No. 2	Sacramento St. bet. California & Pine
June 15, 1850	St. Francis Hook & Ladder Co. No. 3	Dupont St. bet. Sacramento & Clay
June 18, 1850	Lafayette Co. No. 3	Montgomery bet. Jackson & Pacific
June 18, 1850	Sansome Hook & Ladder Co. No. 3	Washington St. bet. Montgomery & Dupont
Sept. 7, 1850	California Co. No. 4	Battery St. nr. Market St.
Sept. 10, 1850	Monumental Co. No. 6	Brenham Place, West Side Plaza
Oct. 17, 1850	Knickerbocker Co. No.5	Merchant St. bet. Montgomery & Kearny
Feb. 22, 1852	Vigilant Co. No. 9	Stockton St. bet. Broadway & Pacific
Sept. 14, 1852	Pennsylvania Co. No.12	Jackson St. bet. Dupont & Kearny
Oct. 12, 1852	Columbia Co. No. 11	Bush St. bet. Kearny & Dupont
Oct. 25, 1852	Crescent Co. No. 10	Pacific St. bet. Montgomery & Dupont
1852-53	Monumental No. 7	
1852-53	Monumental No. 8	

B. FIRE DEPARTMENTS OF SAN FRANCISCO (Cont'd.)

Founded	Name	Location
1853	Brannan Fire Assn.	Halleck nr. Sansome
Aug. 2, 1853	Pacific Co. No. 8	Jackson St. bet. Front & Davis Sts.
Jan. 13, 1854	Manhattan Co. No. 2	Jackson St. bet. Montgomery & Dupont
Feb. 7, 1854	Young America Co. No.13	Mission Dolores
June 17, 1854	Volunteer Co. No. 7	Pine St. bet. Montgomery & Sansome
Feb. 22, 1855	Tiger Co. No. 14	Second St. one door West of Mission St.
1858	Exempt Firemen's Assn.	
1859	Independent Fire Co.	Corner Powell & Eddy Sts.

C. CHURCHES

Founded	Name	Location
1769	St. Francis, Church of Mission Dolores (Roman Church, Rev. R. Flavian (Monk)	
May 20, 1849	1st Presbyterian Church	Occupying the Superior Court Rm., City hall
July 29, 1849	First Congregational Church	Corner Jackson & Virginia Sts.
also listed: July 29, 1849	" " Rev. E. S. Lacey	S. W. cor. California & Dupont
1849	1st Baptist Church	Washington nr. Stockton
Oct. 1849	Lutheran Church (1st Evangelical)	Sutter bet. Dupont and Stockton
1849-50	Methodist Episcopal Rev. Wm. Taylor	Powell St. bet. Washington & Jackson.
1850	Howard St. Church	Howard St. Happy Valley
Sept. 1850	1st Unitarian Church Rev. F. P. Cutler	Stockton St. bet. Clay & Sacramento
1851	Bethel Methodist Episcopal Church Rev. John B. Hill	Mission St. bet. First & Second
1852 City Directory	Catholic Church of St. Francis	Vallejo nr. Dupont
1852	2nd Baptist Church Rev. Wm. Rollinson	Pine St. nr. Montgomery
April, 1852	Congregational Emanuel Synagogue; Pres. Jos. Shamon; Vice Pres. S. Fleishacker; Tres. S. Tilleyer; Sec. E. M. Berg	86 Kearny St.

C.   CHURCHES (Cont'd.)

Founded	Name	Location
1852	Wesley Chapel (Methodist Episcopal) Rev. J. Boring and M. Evans	Powell nr. Clay
1852	Zion Church (Colored) Rev. John Moore	Stockton St. nr. Vallejo
May, 1853	Catholic Church Notre Dame des Victoires	Bush St. bet. Dupont & Stockton
1854	3rd Baptist Church (Colored) Rev. Chas. Satchell	Dupont St. nr. Greenwich
July 17, 1853	St. Mary's Cathedral (Catholic) Most Rev. Archibishop Alemany and Rev. H. P. Gallegher	N. W. cor. Californis & Dupont Sts.
Dec. 15, 1853	Folsom St. Methodist	Bet. First & Second Sts.
July 17, 1854	Calvary Presbyterian Church (Rev. Dr. Scott)	Bush opposite Musical Hall
Aug. 1, 1855	St. Ignatius (Catholic) Rev. F. Maraschi	Market St. Arms' Valley
Sept. 28, 1856	German Methodist Church Rev. Augustus Hertel	N. W. cor. Pine & Dupont Sts.
1856	Bush Street Baptist Church	Bush St. bet. Stockton & Dupont
1856	Chinese Chapel Wm. Speer	Stockton & Sacramento Sts.
1856	Church of God Rev. H. Cummings	Service in Pine St. Chapel nr. Montgomery.
1856	First Christian	4th Dist. Court Rm. City Hall
1856 (reorganized)	African Methodist Episcopal Church (Formerly St. Cyprian Congregation)	Scott St.

C. CHURCHES (Cont'd.)

Founded	Name	Location
1857	St. John's Church Mission Dolores Rev. John Chittenden Pres. San Francisco College	
1858	Welsh Presbyterian Church Rev. D. J. Lewis	Pollard Place Vallejo bet. Dupont & Kearny
April 4, 1858	German Mission Church Rev. Augustus Kellner	Mission St. bet. 3rd & 4th
Dec. 1858 (reorganized)	Methodist Episcopal Church South Rev. O. P. Fitzgerald	Pine St. bet. Montgomery & Kearny
1859	Church of the Advent Rev. F. M. McAllister	Mission St. nr. 2nd
Feb. 20, 1859	German Mission Church Rev. Augustus Kellner	Broadway bet. Stockton & Powell
April 5, 1860	St. Boniface Church (German Roman Catholic)	Sutter St. bet. Kearny & Montgomery
1860-65	Free Chapel of the Holy Innocents	Sutter St. nr. Stockton
	The Congregation Sherith Israel (Hebrew) Rev. D. A. Henry	Bet. Broadway & Vallejo
	German Divine Service Baptist Church Rev. F. Whittenbach	Bush nr. Dupont
	German Evangelical Church 1st Baptist Church Rev. F. Mooshake	Washington St. bet. Stockton & Dupont
	German Methodist Church Rev. Augustus Kellner	N. W. cor. Pine & Dupont
	German Service in 1st Presbyterian Church Rev. F. Mooshake	Stockton bet. Broadway & Pacific
	German Divine Service Rev. A. Kellner	Cor. Bush & Mason

C.   CHURCHES (Cont'd.)

Founded	Name	Location
1860-65	Jewish Synagogue (German)	Broadway nr. Powell
	Mariner's Church	Pacific bet. Front & Davis
	Market Street Methodist Episcopal Church Rev. G. S. Phillips	Residence on Folsom nr. First St.
	Methodist Episcopal Church Pilgrim (Colored) Rev. J. A. Sanderson	Scott St. bet. Pacific & Broadway St.
	Mission Dolores Rev. Richard Carroll	
	New Jerusalem Church James Kellogg, Presiding Officer	Superior Court Rms. of California Exchange
	Notre Dame des Victoires Rev. Dominic Blaive	Bush St. bet. Dupont & Stockton St.
	Olive Branch Baptist	Odd Fellows Hall cor. of Jane & Minna St.
	Seaman's Bethel Rev. Wm. Taylor	Davis St. bet. Clay & Washington St.
	St. Cyprian (African M.E.)	Jackson St. cor. Virginia
	St. Patrick's Church Roman Catholic Rev. John Maginnis	Market St. bet. 2nd & 3rd
	Synagogue (Polish)	Stockton nr. Broadway
	Tabernacle, Baptist Rev. J. B. Saxton	Pine St. nr. Montgomery
	Trinity Episcopal Church	Cor. Jackson & Powell

D. CHORAL SOCIETIES

1851   Althenaeum Club. Met for rehearsals at Athenaeum Build-
       ing. S. E. corner Montgomery and California Streets.

       Die Saenger Am Stillen Meer. Director, Dr. Augustus H.
       Malech.

1852   German Saengerbund. Music Director, Dr. A. H. Malech.
       President, H. Neuhaus.

       Social Turnverein.. Meetings held at Turnverein Hall,
       Bush near Powell. The object of this society is to en-
       courage morality, to improve health, and cultivate mu-
       sic. Number of members, 75, of which about 25 are at-
       tached to the vocal department. President Jacob Weiss;
       First Leader, H. Turk; Second Leader, H. Dieckmann.

1853   Aeolian Vocalists. Organized prior to April, 1853.

       German Turnverein. President, Charles King. Meeting
       place on Vallejo Street, near Stockton. Membership 80,
       of which 30 were in the vocal department.

       Pacific Musical Troupe. Membership, 4. Meeting place,
       Musical Hall, which was built for them.

       Turn und Gesang Verein. Reorganized (?) 1857. Turn-
       verein Society. Rooms, corner of California and Kearny.
       The object of this society is to maintain liberal polit-
       ical and religious principles, to encourage morality,
       to improve health and to cultivate music. Number of
       members, 80, of which about 30 were attached to the vo-
       cal department.

1854   San Francisco Harmonie. Director, Rudolph Herold.
       Meeting place, San Francisco Turn Halle, located at N.
       side Bush between Stockton and Powell. The object of
       this association is for the cultivation and improvement
       of music. Membership, 80, of which 50 were   active
       singers.

1855   Germania Philharmonic. Music Director, Rudolph Herold.

1857   German Glee Club. (Maenner Gesang Verein Eintracht).
       President, F. C. Sack, Leader, P. Reiter. Meeting
       place, rooms of the Lafayette Hook and Ladder Company,
       Broadway. Members, 38.

D. CHORAL SOCIETIES (Cont'd.)

1857   Harmonic Society. Music Director, Rudolph Herold, Membership, 85. President, David S. Turner.

1858   Pacific Saengerbund. Membership, 500. (This was the name of the association of all other choral groups in the city. This organization functioned only on such occasions as the May Festivals and special concerts.)

1859   Cecilien Verein. President, Dr. Regensburger. Director, Rudolph Herold. Membership, 80 of which 30 were ladies, met at the rooms of the San Francisco Verein, 140 Kearny Street, Hunt's Building. President in 1860, F. W. Wedekind. Vice President, H. Neuhaus. (Organized October 2, 1853).

1860   The Twelve. Director, G. A. Scott. Meeting place, rooms at 6 Montgomery Street.

1861   Handel and Haydn Society. Original membership 125 members; in 1863-64 membership increased to 350. Meets for singing every Monday at the vestry of Mr. Lacy's church, corner of Dupont and California Streets. Conductor, G. A. Scott.

Teutonia Mannerchor. President, H. Newman. Music Director. Mr. J. Trenkle, in 1863. Meetings held Monday and Thursday evenings of each week, at Minerva Hall, southwest corner California and Kearny. Number of members, 60.

1862   Thalia Verein. Meetings held in Turnverein. Hall, Bush Street, between Stockton and Powell, on the first and third Tuesday evening in each month. Object: to give dramatic performances and have social reunions. Number of members, 142, of which a majority take an active part in performances.

1865   San Francisco Philharmonic Society. Meetings held quarterly. Rehearsals every Tuesday. Number of members, 25. Object: to promote the cultivation and taste of music. Joseph L. Schmitz, President; Alexander Hildebrand, Secretary.

1866   San Francisco Chorus Society. Organized prior to 1866.

E. ORCHESTRAS AND BANDS

CONCERT ORCHESTRAS

1852-55   San Francisco Philharmonic, George Loder, Conductor.
1855-60   Germania Philharmonic. Usually associated with the Turnverein; conducted by Rudolph Herold from 1855 to 1860; later by A. Reiff Jr.

THEATRE ORCHESTRAS

1853   Chinese Dramatic Company Orchestra.
1854-56   Metropolitan Theatre Orchestra; Robert Nicholas Bochsa, Conductor.
1858   Maguire's Opera House Orchestra; George Koppitz, Conductor.
1863   Jenny Lind Theatre Orchestra; George H.Williams, Conductor.
1864   New Idea Theatre Orchestra; George H.Edmonds, L. Mundwiler, and Harry Williams, Conductors.
1864   American Theatre Orchestra; Napier Lothian, Conductor.

CHAMBER ORCHESTRAS

1853   Verandah Concert Society, performed at Verandah Hall from 1853 to 1855.
1853   Miska Hauser's Quartette.
1856   Quartette under the direction of Herr Sneider.
1856   Trio under the direction of Jacques Blumenthal.

ORCHESTRA CONDUCTORS

1852   George Loder conducted the San Francisco Philharmonic. Signor Bona directed a benefit concert for Eliza Biscaccianti at the American Theatre; also conducted at Musical Hall in 1854.
1854   Rudolph Herold conducted Germania Philharmonic.
1856   Charles Kohler directed concert of the Amateur Musical Club at Musical Hall.
1857   C. A. Andres music director at Turnverein May Festival.
1858   G.A. Scott directed promenade concert at Musical Hall.
1863   Louis Schmidt directed concert at Platt's New Music Hall.

BRASS BANDS

1853   Herr Kohler's Union Band.
1854   Union Brass Band played at Turnverein dedication.
1855   Union Cornet Band played at May Festival of Turnverein.
1855   Croome's Band.

E.   ORCHESTRAS AND BANDS (Cont'd.)

BRASS BANDS (Cont'd.)

1856	German Brass Band; Ferdinand Pape, Leader.
1856	Kohler's Brass Band.
1857	San Francisco Brass Band; 6 men mounted, in Admission Day Parade.
1857	American Brass Band; 16 men in gray uniforms with bear-skin caps in Admission Day and Washington's Birthday Parades. A. Wolcott, Leader.
1859	Germania Band played at May Festival; Buechel, Leader.
1861	Germanic Cotillion Band; furnished music for Washington's Birthday celebration at Platt's New Music Hall; Charles Andres, Leader.
1863	Excelsior Brass Band at Willow's Gardens. Band of the Ninth Regiment with J.W. Fuller's Quadrille Band of 14 pieces, played for Washington's Birthday celebration at Platt's Hall.
1864	Second Regimental Brass Band. McClellan Brass Band at Willows Gardens.

F.   OPERA COMPANIES

Most Popular Operas: (1850-1860)

Title	Performances
La Fille Du Regiment	23
Norma	18
The Crown Diamonds	18
La Sonnambula	17
Fra Diavolo	12

Most Popular Houses

Name	Performances
First Metropolitan	162
Maguire's Opera House	83
The Second American	35
Adelphi	20

Opera Repertoire   (1850-1860)

Opera	Performances
La Sonnambula	17
Norma	18
Ernani	11
La Fille du Regiment	23
La Favorita	9
La Dame Blanche	3
Gilles Ravasseur	3
The Barber of Seville	9
The Crown Diamonds	18
The Black Domino	2
The Enchantress	8
The Bohemian Girl	11
Lucia di Lammermoor	6
Il Maestro de Capella	2
Don Pasquale	7
Cinderella	12
Pride of the Harem	1
Linda di Chamounix	2
Lucrezia Borgia	12
Der Freischutz	12
Judith	6
Martha	10
Jeanette's Wedding	3
Nabuco	3
Maria di Rohan	3
Fra Diavolo	12

Opera Repertoire (1850-1860) (Cont'd.)

Opera	Performances
Black-eyed Susan	1
Robert le Diable	7
L'Elisir d'Amore	4
Don Giovanni	3
I Due Foscari	3
Creation	2
Bonsoir, Voisin	1
I Lombardi	3
La Gazza Ladra	2
La Muette di Portici	1
Il Trovatore	12
Le Cid	1
Attila	3
Beggar's Opera	3
Pocahontas	2
John of Paris	3
Midas	4
Rob Roy	4
La Traviata	2
Marriage of Figaro	

G: MINSTRELS

Date	Name	Place

1849

| Oct. 22 | Philadelphia Minstrels (1st Minstrel Performance) | Bella Union Hall |

1850

| Jan. 16 | Pacific Minstrels | Washington Hall |
| Feb. 9 | Virginia Serenaders | Washington Hall |

1851

| Jan. & Feb. | Sable Harmonists | 1st Jenny Lind |

1852

Feb. to July	Buckley's New Orleans Serenaders	Adelphi Theatre Dupont Street 3rd Jenny Lind
March & June	Rainier & Donaldson Minstrels	1st American
July 11-25	J. C. Rainier's Operatic Serenaders	1st American
Nov. 15-22	Campbell's Minstrels	Armory Hall

1853

Jan. 15 to Feb. 28	Buckley's New Orleans Serenaders	Armory Hall
Apr. 1 to 10 Apr. 14 to 17	Buckley's New Orleans Serenaders with Dramatic Troupe	First American Armory Hall
May 16-21	Sable Harmonists (2nd Troupe)	Adelphi Theatre Dupont Street
July 11 to Aug. 27	Tracy's Minstrels	Adelphi Theatre Dupont Street
Sept. 21 to Oct. 3	Donnelly's Minstrels (Name changed to San Francisco Minstrels)	Adelphi Theatre
Oct. 3	San Francisco Minstrels	Adelphi Theatre Dupont Street

G: <u>MINSTRELS</u>   (Cont'd.)

<u>1853</u>

Oct. 9	San Francisco Minstrels		American Theatre
Dec. 12	" " "		Adelphi Theatre

<u>1855</u>

April 21 to May 15	"	"	"	San Francisco Hall
May 26 to June 3	"	"	"	1st Metropolitan
June 6	"	"	"	San Francisco Hall
Aug. 5	"	"	"	1st Metropolitan S. F. Hall
Sept. 14-26	"	"	"	San Francisco Hall
Dec. 6-30	"	"	"	San Francisco Hall

<u>1856</u>

Jan. 11 to Feb. 3	"	"	"	San Francisco Hall
Mar. 9 to Apr. 15	"	"	"	San Francisco Hall
Apr. 19	"	"	"	1st Metropolitan
Apr. 21	"	"	"	San Francisco Hall
June 9	"	"	"	1st Metropolitan
June 11	"	"	"	San Francisco Hall
June 12	"	"	"	1st Metropolitan
June 13-22				San Francisco Hall

<u>1854</u>

Jan. 24 to Jan. 10, <u>1855</u>	Backus Minstrels	San Francisco Hall

<u>1856</u>

July 6	San Francisco Minstrels and Backus Minstrels combined.	San Francisco Hall
July 25	-do-	1st Metropolitan
July 27	-do-	San Francisco Hall

G: MINSTRELS (Cont'd.)

1856

Aug. 13	San Francisco Minstrels & Backus Minstrels combined.	1st Metropolitan
Aug. 16	-do-	San Francisco Hall
Oct. 8	-do-	1st Metropolitan
Oct. 13	-do-	San Francisco Hall
Oct. 19	-do-	Last night of the season.

1857

Apr. 20	San Francisco Minstrels	Maguire's Opera House
May 25 to June 30	" " "	(Formerly S.F. Hall) Maguire's Opera House
July 12 to Aug. 2	" " "	-do-
July 28	" " "	1st Metropolitan
Aug. 14	" " "	" "
Aug. 18 to Sept. 20	" " "	Maguire's Opera House
Oct. 20 to Nov. 8	" " "	-do-
Dec. 20 to Dec. 28	" " "	-do-

1854

Oct. 23	E. P. Christy's Minstrels	Music Hall

1855

Jan.23 to Apr. 8	Christy & Backus Minstrels	San Francisco Hall
July 14	Lone Star Serenaders (Winn's) closed at end of week.	Winn's Saloon
Aug. 27	Metropolitan Minstrels (Corrister's)	Corner Merchant and Kearny
Sept. 2	-do- (ended)	-do-

1856

Mar. 7	Eph Horn's Minstel Entertainment	2nd American

G: <u>MINSTRELS</u> (Cont'd.)

1856

Sept. 17-25	California Minstrels	Union Theatre
Nov. 29	" "	Maguire's Opera House
Dec. 22	" "	-do-
Dec. 28	" "	-do-

1857

Jan. 3 to	California Minstrels	Maguire's Opera
Mar. 1		House
Feb. 2	Max Zorer's Minstrels	2nd American
Mar. 2	" " "	Union Theatre
Mar. 8	" " "	" "
May 20	" " " and	2nd American
	Burlesque Entertainment	
Feb. 23 to	Virginia Minstrels	Concert Hall
Mar. 1		
Mar. 2-15	Wood's Minstrels	" "

1858

Apr. 10	California Minstrels com-bined with Pennsylvanians	Melodeon
June 7 to	-do-	Lyceum
Aug. 20		
Apr. 16-18	San Francisco Minstrels	Maguire's Opera House
June 7 to	George Christy's Minstrels	-do-
July 25		
Sept. 13 to	" " "	-do-
Oct. 17		
Dec. 6-20	" " "	2nd American
Dec. 25	Lyceum Minstrel & Burlesque Company	Lyceum

1859

Jan. 2-24	Lyceum Minstrel & Burlesque Company	Lyceum
Apr. 30	-do-	2nd American
May 8-18	San Francisco Minstrels	Maguire's Opera House
July 2-19	Wells & Hussey's Minstrels	Lyceum
July 29	" " "	2nd American
Aug. 6	Wells & Coe's Minstrels	" "
Sept. 5	H. Donnelly's Minstrel & Dramatic Benefit	Lyceum

G: <u>MINSTRELS</u> (Cont'd.)

<u>1859</u>

Sept. 27 to Oct. 20	Billy Birch's Minstrels	Maguire's Opera House
Dec. 25	" " "	Music Hall 181 Washington St.

<u>1860</u>

Jan. 20	Birch & Well's Minstrels	Maguire's Opera House
Jan. 28 to Feb. 23	" " "	Athenaeum
Mar. 9-16	" " "	"
Apr. 3-8	Birch & Murphy's Minstrels	Maguire's Opera House
Apr. 22	Billy Birch's Minstrels	Music Hall
May 9	" " "	Maguire's Opera House
May 10	" " "	Music Hall
June 13-19	Birch's Ethiopian Opera Troupe	Tucker's Academy

H: MUSIC TEACHERS

1850	Denham, S. H.	Parker House
	Sangrado, Manuel	Broadway, bet. Sansome & Dupont
	Truper, Andrew	Stockton bet. Broadway & Virginia
1856	Bohme, F.	Clara Street near Bush Street
	Buchel, E.	Turn Verein Hall, Bush Street
	Carnand, J.	181 Commercial Street
	Chamberlain, I.	Broadway bet. Stockton & Dupont
	Cramer, H.	Sutter bet. Montgomery & Stockton
	Dean, John	Carswell House, Stockton near Clay
	Fischer, A.	Meyer's Hotel
	Fischer, C.	256 Stockton Street
	Frohling, John	256 Stockton Street
	Fuller, J. U.	124 Bush Street
	Hildebrand, A.	256 Stockton Street
	Jork, Charles	Turn Verein Hall, Bush Street
	Kendall, Charles	256 Stockton Street
	Kohler, Charles	256 Stockton Street
	Koppitz, C.	533 Union Street
	Loder, George	256 Stockton Street
	Roach, F.	
	Schutz, E.	Turn Verein Hall, Bush Street
	Simonsen, Martin	Dupont Street opposite Commercial Street
	Smith, Joseph	Pine Street near Dupont
	Tyte, E.	226 Stockton Street
	Werther, C.	Post Street near Stockton
	Waldo, G. Mrs.	Stockton near Union
	Winter, Clinton	Dupont near Union
1858	Armstrong, Jane, Miss	262 Pacific
	Bowers, J. T.	Stevenson bet. 3rd & 4th Streets
	Barnard, Jules	181 Commercial Street
	Deliajie, M. Mrs.	198 California Street
	Ferrer, M.	Cor. Sacramento & Brooklyn Place
	Frederick, M.	156 Sacramento Street
	Herrold, R.	109 Merchant Street
	Hering, W.	117 Bush Street
	Lawless, M. Miss	Montgomery near Vallejo
	Levison, C. Mrs.	Cor. Vallejo and Maiden Lane
	Loundes, A. L.	Bush near Mason
	Nichols, P. R.	18 Sansome Street
	Pettinos, G. F.	426 Second Street
	Pioda, Paul	164 Commercial Street
	Pique, E.	172 Washington Street
	Planel, L. T.	258 Stockton Street
	Planel, H. Mme.	258 Stockton Street
	Richter, H. W. Miss	Green near Dupont
	Spencer, Mrs.	Pine near Mary Lane
	Scott, G. A.	282 Clay Street

H: <u>MUSIC TEACHERS</u> (Cont'd.)

<u>1859</u>	Armstrong, Mary	Tehama near First Street
	Blanchard, Mrs. C. D.	Ellis near Stockton Street
	Lapfgeer, A.	220 Dupont Street
	Lepper, Miss	Cor. Bush and Taylor Street
	Levinson, C. Mr.	Powell and Green Street
	McKorkell, W.	190 California Street
	Rasche, H.	650 Washington Street
	Stadefeld, C.	Vallejo near Stockton
<u>1860</u>	Alfers, C.	Cor. Sacramento & Kearny Streets
	Andres, C.	84 Kearny Street
	Barry, Mrs. Teresa	Hubbard near Howard Street
	Bauman, J.	29th. Street Marks Place
	Crapeaux, C.	103 Broadway Street
	Dowling, H. Mrs.	Howard near Second
	Eaton, M. L. Miss	Cor. Pine and Jones Streets
	Ferch, F.	101 Dupont Street
	Kallitz, W. Mrs.	Market near Third Street
	Leach, Stephen, W.	610 Mason Street
	Mitchell, F. K.	Public Schools
<u>1861</u>	Casenova, C. Miss	1114 Powell Street
	Cassin, M. F. Miss	46 Natoma
	Cohen, Waldow, Mme.	1505 Stockton
	Curties, M. L. Mrs.	Washington & Dupont
	Dias, C. Mrs. (Piano)	1114 Powell Street
	Elliott, W.	N. E. corner Broadway & Polk Streets
	Evans, G. T.	N. E. corner Broadway & Polk Streets
	Griswold, Anna	518 Bush Street
	Hale, E. A. Mrs.	1018 Stockton Street
	Hecht, L. Mrs.	1314 Dupont Street
	Hilmers, N. S.	919 Powell Street
	Mueller, C.	828 Vallejo Street
	O'Keefe, Louise Frances	9 Post Street
	Rasche, F.	650 Washington
	Rollina, R.	835 Dupont Street
	Weston, A.	916 Green Street
<u>1862</u>	Anderson, M. A.	72 Natoma Street
	Brenner, C.	443 Bush Street
	Clemons, S. G. Mrs.	548 Mission Street
	Hasback, E. Mrs.	714 Green Street
	Lunr, E. M. Miss	72 Natoma Street
	Morris, K. Miss	1217 Powell Street
	Oliphant, H. D. Mrs.	812 Bush Street
	Schmidt, Louis	260 O'Farrell Street
	Schmitz, J. L.	515 Howard Street
	Shully, G.	211 Post Street
	Trenkle, J.	653 Howard Street
<u>1863</u>	Allen, J.	912 Market Street
	Anthes, F. T.	St. Mary Place

H: <u>MUSIC TEACHERS</u> (Cont'd.)

<u>1863</u>	Coad, S.	561 Mission Street
	Daggett, E. Mrs.	313 Union Street
	Enrich, E.	615 Commercial Street
	Kidd, A.	Post near Mason
	Liebert, B.	630 Sacramento Street
	Striby, L. Mrs.	679 Mission Street
	Touissin, E.	2 St. Mary
	Williams, E. Miss	1017 Mason Street
<u>1864</u>	Barrette, M. E.	49 Clementina Street
	Beutler, J. B.	13 Natoma Street
	Catano, M.	650 Washington Street
	Dohrmann, J. H.	337 Bush Street
	Emerson, R. Mrs.	230 O'Farrell Street
	Gage, M. A. Miss	329 Minna Street
	Guidon, I.	910 Stockton Street
	Hartmann, E.	522 Dupont Street
	Hooker, L. Mrs.	3 Monroe Street
	Kemp, E. Miss	155 Third Street
	Kuhne, A.	731 California Street
	Larkin, C.	845 Dupont Street
	Martini, L. A.	917 Sacramento Street
	Sprigue, M. Mrs.	731 Clay Street
	Washburn, M. A.	624 Market Street
	Willey, M. B.	626 California Street

I: VISITING CELEBRITIES

1849

June 22	Massett, Steve, vocalist	First Concert

1850

Mar. 26	Hertz, Henri, pianist	
Oct. 30	Von Gulpen, Mme., vocalist	First Jenny Lind

1851

Jan. 28	Pellegrini, Signor & Signora	Operatic Concert at Adelphi
June 18	Faubert, Mme., French vocalist	Second Jenny Lind
Sept. 7	Koska, Mme. vocalist	Adelphi (Dupont)

1852

Mar. 22	Biscaccianti, Elisa Mme.	First Concert (Dir., George Loder)
Nov. 30	Hayes, Kate	First Concert (American Theatre)

1853

Jan. 3	Pettinos, F. Mr., pianist	S. F. Hall
Feb. 9	Hauser, Miska	First Concert (S. F. Hall)
Apr. 13	Koppitz, flutist	First appearance (S. F. Hall)
June 4	Cheval, Chas. Mons.	Farewell Concert (Adelphi, Dupont)
June 18	Bruce, Ella, Miss	First Concert (Adelphi Hall)
July 16	Potier, Mme.	252 Dupont St.
July 26	"Pacific Musical Troupe" Laura A. Jones Messrs. J. Butler I. C. Smith Miss M. Leach G. Loder, Conductor. Signor	
July 28	Abalos, & Daughter.	Musical Hall Concert
Aug. 13	Herold, R. & Koppitz, Chas.	Musical Hall Concert
Sept. 13	Hauser, Miska & Pique Robb, Mrs. (nee Goodenow)	First Concert (Union Theatre)
Nov. 29	Waller, Mrs.	Farewell Concert (Musical Hall)

1854

Jan. 16	Hudson, Mr.	1st Appearance
Jan. 16	Leach, S. W.	1st Appearance
Jan. 16	Thillon, Anna Mme.	1st Appearance
Feb. 2	Bishop, Madam Anna & Bochsa (Harpist)	Arrived from the East.
Feb. 7	Bishop, Anna	1st Concert (Musical Hall)

I: VISITING CELEBRITIES (Cont'd.)

1854			
Feb.	7	Bochsa,	1st Appearance
Mar.	6	Abalos, Signora & daughters, Sophia and Caroline	Concert. Corner Stockton and Jackson Streets
Mar.	14	Thillon, Mr. C.	1st Appearance Metropolitan
Mar.	29	Frery, Miss	1st Appearance Metropolitan
Apr.	2	Cailli, Mme.	Arrived from the East
June	1	Patti, Carlotta Mme.(Vocalist)	Union Theatre
June	13	"Mountaineers" Julia Gould, Marie Leach, S. W. Leach, L.T. Zander, L. C. Smith	First Concert Musical Hall
July	1	Strakosch, Maurice (Pianist)	
July	15	Bull, Ole (Violinist)	Metropolitan
July	24	Bull, Ole (Violinist)	Metropolitan
July	26	Bull, Ole & Strakosch, M.	Metropolitan 2nd Concert
Sept.	18	Ferrar, Don Manuel (Guitarist)	Metropolitan 1st Appearance
Nov.	14	Thorne, Barili Mme.	Metropolitan 1st Appearance
1855			
Mar.	2	Patti, Carlotta Mme.(Pianist)	Metropolitan 1st Appearance
July	24	Leach, S. W.	Metropolitan Farewell Ben.
Sept.	2	Van Des Broeck, Josephine	Musical Hall 1st Appearance
Oct.	9	Garbato, Mme. Prima Donna Garbato, Signor (Conductor	
Nov.	3	Garbato, Drusilla Signora)	Musical Hall 1st Concert
Nov.	16	Massett, Steve	Metropolitan Benefit Concert
Nov.	22	Simonson, J. A.	Musical Hall Farewell benefit Concert
1856			
Nov.	19	Hegelund, Amanda (Vocalist)	Musical Hall 1st Appearance
1857			
Jan.	6	McKorkell, Mr. (Harpist)	American Theatre Concert
Feb.	9	Donnelly, J. J. (Vocalist)	Union Theatre 1st Appearance
Apr.	21	Kelley, John (Violinist)	Melodeon. 1st appearance after 6 years absence.

I: <u>VISITING CELEBRITIES</u> (Cont'd.)

<u>1857</u>

May 9	Ince, Caroline (Vocalist)	Metropolitan 1st Appearance
Aug. 1	Mironda, Miss (Vocalist)	Opera House 1st Appearance
Oct. 7	Wheaton, J. B. (Pianist)	Opera House 1st Appearance

<u>1858</u>

Apr. 29	Poncini, Signor	Musical Hall Concert
June 3	Leach, S. W.	1st Appearance after his return.
June 3	Griswold, Anna	Musical Hall 1st Appearance
Aug. 9	Leach, S. W. and Mrs.G.S.Leach	Musical Hall 1st Appearance
Oct. 23	Bianchi, Signor & Signora	Opera House 1st of series of operatic concerts. 1st Appearance

<u>1859</u>

Aug. 11	Locher, E. Hass	Musical Hall 1st Appearance
Aug. 11	Waklaw, E. (Violinist)	Musical Hall
Oct. 13	Evans, George T. (Pianist)	Arrived from the East.
Nov. 4	States, Agatha	Musical Hall Concert
Nov. 9	Massett, Steve	Musical Hall 1st Concert & Entertainment since his return.
Dec. 31	Evans, George T., Feret Mme.,	Lyceum Musical Soiree

<u>1860</u>

Feb. 11	Biscaccianti, Mme.	Opera House Matinee Concert
Feb. 17	Staderman, Charles (Violinist)	Academy of Music. Concert 1st Appearance
Mar. 16	Oakley, C. R. (Violinist)	Atheneum 1st Appearance
May 5	Connor, John W. (Irish Vocalist)	Opera House 1st Appearance
May 5	Hammersmith, Miss J. (Vocalist)	Opera House 1st Appearance
Nov. 14	Howard, Emma Miss (Vocalist)	Apollo 1st Appearance

J: COMPOSERS AND WORKS

Date	Composer	Work
1849	Rhodes, Charles	"The Days of Old, The Days of Gold, and The Days of '49."
1855	Atwill & Co. Pub.	"The California Pioneers." (The first piece of music published in California.)
	Baker, Thomas	"Katy-did Song."
	Brown, Charles H.	"Polka."
	Christy, E.	"We Are Coming Sister Mary."
	Jarvis, C.	"Music Murmurings in the Trees."
	Lachner	"The Lotus Flower."
	Massett, Stephen C.	"You're All the World to Me."
		"When the Moon on the Lake is Beaming."
		"When a Child I Roamed."
		"List While I Sing."
		"Clear The Way."
		"I'll Wait For Thee Mary."
	Noisy Carrier, Pub., 77 Long Wharf	"A California Song Book." Composer unknown, possession of De Young Museum, San Francisco.
	Voss, Charles (Arr.)	"Carnival of Venice," by Paganini.
	Wallace, Vincent	"Say My Heart, Can This Be Love?"
	Wurgil	"The Song of The Old Hall Clock."
1856	Garbato, Signor	"The Firemen's March." Dedicated to the San Francisco Fire Department.
	Koppitz, Christian (Arr.)	"Nightingale Waltz." Arranged for piano. "Carnival of Venice." by Ernst, arranged for flute.
1857	White, Clement	"Where Shall We Meet?"
1858	Jeffreys, Charles.(Words) Croall, George (Music)	"The Lonely Watches." Lancer's Quadrille.
	McDonald, D. F. (Words) Nichols, P. R. (Music)	"Jennie My Darling."

J: <u>COMPOSERS AND WORKS</u> (Cont'd.)

<u>Date</u>	Composer	Work
<u>1858</u>	Payot, Henry Pub. Composer unknown.	"Dernieres Chanson de Beranger."
<u>1859</u>	McKorkell, W.	"Fleur De Marie." Military Polka.
	Nicholls, P. R.	"Millie of the Vale." "Florence Fay." (Ballads)
	Phillips, Henry (Words) McKorkell, W. (Music)	"Rosy Hannah." (Ballad)
	Planel, L. T.	"'Tis Always Sad to Part."
<u>1860</u>	Soule, Frank (Words) McKorkell, W. (Music)	"Gentle Mary Hand."
	St. Clair, C. G.	"The Octaroon." (Song) "Of These My Thoughts are Fondly Dwelling." (Song)
<u>1862</u>	Evans, George T.	"Minnie Adair." (Ballad)
	Rimbault, Edw. F.	"Bright Things Can Never Die." (Ballad)
<u>1863</u>	Bray, Walter (Words) Corrister, W. D. (Music)	"An Hour at the Cliff." (Ballad) Arranged by Geo. H. Edmonds.

K: INSTRUMENT MAKERS

PIANO FORTE

Year	Name	Address
1849	Falkenberg, J. H.	Jackson Street
1856	Allovan, J. D.	Stone & Jackson Street
1857	Bender, John	3 Post Street
	Zech, Jacob	111 Clay Street
1859	Zech, Jacob	529 California Street
1862	Woodworth, Allovan & Co.	12 Post Street
	Zech, Frederick	2 Summer Street

STRINGED INSTRUMENTS

1857	Stumcke, Charles	Violins & Guitars 140 Sacramento Street
	Urban, Joseph	Violins & Guitars Corner of Kearny & St. Mark's Place
1860	Morrell, Charles	Banjos, 150 Sansome Street
	Mojica, D.	Guitars, Kearny Street

ACCORDIONS

1862	Keene, C. C.	Flutinas & Accordions 103 Montgomery Street

FLUTES AND CLARINETS

1860	Plaff, George	203 Washington Street

PIANO TUNERS AND REPAIRERS

1854	Cramer, Prof. H.	With Atwill & Co. 172 Washington Street
1860	Hodges, S.	With Gray & Herwig 163 Clay Street
1862	Geib, H.	With Badger & Lindenberger, 413 Battery Street

ORGAN BUILDERS

1858	Farran, Robert	Powell nr. Green Street
	McCraith, John	Broadway & Hyde Sts.
1859	Shellard, B.	Montgomery nr. Green St.
1861	Mayer, Joseph	728 Montgomery St.
1862	Woodworth, Allovan & Co.	12 Post Street
1863	Pierce, W. S.	26 Montgomery Street

L: MUSIC DEALERS

ATWILL & COMPANY
1850	Located on Plaza in old Zinc Building.
1851	Moved to 172 Washington Street.

A. KOHLER MUSIC STORE
1850	Small store opened at foot of Broadway.
1852	Moved to 276 Stockton Street.
1857	New Branch Store opened at 178 Washington Street.
1859	Second Branch opened at 424 Sansome Street.
1861	Stores at 178 Washington Street and 276 Stockton Street discontinued; larger stores opened at 630 Washington Street and 1108 Stockton Street.
1863	Moved to 620 Washington Street.

MARVIN & HITCHCOCK
1852	168 Montgomery Street
1855	Succeeded by E. G. Hall. Same address.

SALVATOR ROSA
1852	180 Clay Street.
1856	Moved to 193 Clay Street.
1858	Moved to 157 Montgomery Street.
1861	Moved to 615 Montgomery Street.

Woodworth & Company
1852	Located in Corinthian Building at 130 Clay Street.
1856	Moved to 16 Montgomery Street.
1861	Moved to 28 Montgomery Street.
1862	Became Woodworth-Allovan & Co., located in Masonic Temple at 12 Post Street.

WILLIAM G. BADGER
1856	101-3-5 Battery Street.
1858	Became Badger & Lindenberger.
1861	Moved to 411-13-15 Battery Street.

RASCHE & PFLEUGER
1856	190 Washington Street.
1859	Became Rasche & Sons. Same address.
1861	Moved to 650 Washington Street.
1862	Moved to 131 Montgomery Street.
1863	Became Rasche Bros. Same address.

DODGE & EDOURT
1856	112 Sacramento Street.

L: MUSIC DEALERS (Cont'd.)

JOHN T. PIDWELL
1858   140 Washington Street.

FRESE & COMPANY
1859   51 Commercial Street.

GRAY & HERWIG
1859   176 Clay Street.
1860   163 Clay Street.
1861   Became M. Gray Co., at 613 Clay Street.

P. MAURY JR.
1859   710 Sansome Street.

DR. E. R. SMILIE
1859   161 Montgomery Street.

JOHN T. BOWERS
1863   131 Montgomery Street.

HEYER & COMPANY
1863   206 Battery Street.
1864   Moved to 406 Battery Street.

W. S. PIERCE
1863   26 Montgomery Street.

FELDBUSH & COMPANY
1864   Russ House Block.

M: MUSIC PUBLISHERS

Year	Name	Address
1855	Atwill & Company	172 Washington Street.
1857	Kohler, A. & Co.	276 Stockton Street.
1859	Rasche & Sons	190 Washington Street.
1862	Gray, M. & Co.	613 Clay Street.
1862	Rosa, Salvator	615 Montgomery Street.
1864	Bowers, J. T.	131 Montgomery Street.

MUSIC OF THE GOLD RUSH ERA
BIBLIOGRAPHY

CHAPTER I.

Bancroft, Robert Howe. History of California (San Francis-
co: A. L. Bancroft and Co., 1884).
Bolton, Herbert Eugene. Anza's California Expeditions, 1774,
1776 (Berkeley: University of California Press, 1930).
Dobie, Charles Caldwell. San Francisco: A Pageant (New
York: D. Appleton-Century Co., 1933).
Dwinelle, John Whipple. The Colonial History Of San Francis-
co (San Francisco: Towne and Bacon, 1863).
Eldredge, Zoeth Skinner. The Beginnings of San Francisco
(San Francisco: Zoeth S. Eldredge, 1912).
Engelhardt, Father Zephyrin. The Missions and Missionaries
of California (San Francisco: The J. H. Barry Co., 1908).
Engelhardt, Father Zephyrin. San Francisco or Mission Dolor-
es (Chicago: Franciscan Herald Press, 1924).
Palou, Francisco Fr. Life of Junipero Serra and Noticias
(San Francisco: P. E. Dougherty Co., 1884).
Palou, Francisco Fr. New California (Berkeley: University
of California Press, 1926).
Powers, Stephen. Tribes of California (Washington: Govern-
ment Printing Office, 1877).
Saunders, Charles Francis, and Chase, J. Smeaton. The Cali-
fornia Padres and Their Missions (New York: Houghton,
Mifflin Co., 1915).
Soulé, Frank and Nisbet, James, and Gihon, John H. Annals of
San Francisco (New York: D. Appleton and Co., 1855).
Young, John P. San Francisco, A History of the Pacific Coast
Metropolis (San Francisco: The S. J. Clarke Publishing
Co., 1912) Vol. 1.

CHAPTER II.

Bancroft, Hubert Howe. History of California (San Francis-
co: A. L. Bancroft and Co., 1884).
Blackmar, Frank Wilson. Spanish Institutions of the South-
west (Baltimore: John Hopkins Press, 1891).
Briones, Brigida. "A Glimpse of Domestic Life in 1827"
(Century Magazine)
Clark, Galen. Indians of the Yosemite Valley and Vicinity
(San Francisco: H. S. Crocker Co.,   ).
Dana, Richard. Two Years Before the Mast (Boston: Houghton,
Mifflin and Co., 1869).
Davis, William Heath. Sixty Years in California (San Fran-
cisco: A. J. Leary, 1889).
Dwinelle, John Whipple. The Colonial History of San Francis-
co (San Francisco: Towne and Bacon, 1863).
Engelhardt, Father Zephyrin. The Missions and Missionaries
of California (San Francisco: The J. H. Barry Co., 1908).

CHAPTER II. (Cont'd.)

Hague, Eleanor; Ross, Gertrude. Early Spanish-California Folk Songs (New York: Fischer and Co., 1922).

Kotzebue, Otto von. Voyage of Discovery in the South Sea (London: Sir Richard Phillips and Co., 1821).

La Perouse, Jean François de Galaup. Voyage Round the World translation. (London: J. Johnson, 1798).

Mofras, Eugene Duflot de. Explorations du territoire de L'Oregon et Californias (Paris: A. Bertrand, 1844).

Lummis, Charles F. Spanish Songs of the Spanish Sierras (New York: G. Schirmer Co., 1923).

Robinson, Alfred. Life in California (New York: Wiley and Putnam, 1846; San Francisco: W. Doxey, 1891; San Francisco: T. O. Russell, 1925).

Sanchez, Nellie Van de Grift. California and Californians, Hispanic Period (Chicago: B. F. Lewis Co., 1926).

Sanchez, Nellie Van de Grift. Spanish Arcadia (San Francisco-Los Angeles-Chicago: Powell Publishing Co., 1929).

Shinn, Charles Howard. "Ranch and Mission Days in Alta California" (Ed. by Charles Howard Shinn from notes obtained from Guadalupe Vallejo. Century Magazine,) Vol. XIX.

CHAPTER III.

Asbury, Herbert. Barbary Coast, The (New York: Alfred A. Knopf, 1933).

Bancroft, Hubert Howe. California Inter Pocula (San Francisco: The History Co., 1888).

Barry, T. A. and Patten, B. A. Men and Memories of San Francisco in the Spring of '50 (San Francisco: A. B. Bancroft and Co., 1873).

Chamberlain, Newell G. The Call of Gold (Mariposa, California: Gazette Press, 1936).

de Massey, Ernest. A Frenchman in the Gold Rush Translated by Marguerite Eyer Wilbur. (San Francisco: California Historical Society Quarterly, 1927).

de Russailh, Albert Benard. Last Adventure Translated by Clarkson, Crane. (San Francisco: Westgate Press, 1931; Grabhorn Press, 1931- 475 copies).

Dobie, Charles Caldwell. San Francisco A Pageant (New York; London: D. E. Appleton-Century Co., 1933).

Doxey, William. Guide to San Francisco and the Pleasure Resorts of California (San Francisco: 1897).

Eldredge, Zoeth Skinner. The Beginnings of San Francisco (San Francisco: Zoeth S. Eldredge, 1912).

CHAPTER III. (Cont'd.)

Grey, William. Pioneer Times in San Francisco (San Francisco 1881).

Jacobson, Pauline. Articles in the San Francisco Bulletin, 1917.

Knower, Daniel. Adventures of a Forty-Niner (New York: Reed & Parsons Printing Co., 1894).

Lloyd, Benjamin Estelle. Lights and Shades of San Francisco (San Francisco A. L. Bancroft and Co., 1876).

Lomax, John A. Cowboy Songs and Other Frontier Ballads (New York: The MacMillan Co., 1936).

Metzger, Alfred. Pacific Coast Musical Review (San Francisco: October, 1907).

Phillips, Catherine Coffin. Portsmouth Plaza (San Francisco John Henry Nash, 1932).

Shay, Frank. Deep Sea Shanties, Old Sea Songs Heinman, Wm. Ed. (London: London Press, 1935).

Taylor, Bayard. El Dorado, or Adventures in the Path of Empire (New York: George P. Putnam and Co., 1850).

Taylor, Rev. William. Seven Years' Street Preaching in San Francisco (New York: Carlton & Porter, 1856).

Vilas, Martin S. The Barbary Coast of San Francisco (San Francisco: 1915) Pamphlet

CHAPTER IV.

Bates, D. B. Mrs., Four Years on the Pacific Coast (Boston. J. French & Co., 1860).

de Russailh, Albert B. Last Adventure Translated by Clarkson : Crane. (San Francisco: Westgate Press, 1931).

Hittel, John S. Resources of California (San Francisco: A. Roman and Co., 1866).

Massett, Stephen C. Article in the California Historical Quarterly. Vol. 15, p. 45.

Neville, A. R. Fantastic City (New York: Houghton-Mifflin Co., 1932).

Saxon, Isabelle. Five Years Within the Golden Gate (London. Chapman and Hall, 1868).

Soulé, Frank; Nisbet, James; Gihon, John H. Annals of San Francisco: (New York: D. Appleton Co., 1855).

Tevis, A. H. Rev., Beyond the Sierras (Philadelphia: J. P. Lippincott, 1877).

Wide West, 1854; April 27, 1857, March 21, 1858).

San Francisco Call, (San Francisco, 1858).

Young, John P. San Francisco, A History of the Pacific Coast Metropolis (San Francisco: The S. J. Clarke Publishing Co., 1912).

CHAPTER V.

Taylor, William D. D. Seven Years' of Street Preaching in San
Francisco Ed. by W. P. Strickland. (New York: Carlton and
Porter, 200 Mulberry Street; entered by D. L. Ross, 1856).

Newspapers and Periodicals:

San Francisco Bulletin Articles written by "100" (San Francisco: Feb. 27, July 8, Aug. 5, Aug. 11, Oct. 6,   1856).

CHAPTER VI.

Colville, Samuel. Colville's Directory, 1856-1857 (San Fran-
cisco: Commercial Steam Presses, 1857).
Langley, Henry G. San Francisco Directory for Year 1858 (San
Francisco: S. D. Valentine and Son, Commercial Steam Press)
McCabe, Joseph. Diary Unpublished. (San Francisco: Sutro
Branch, State Library). 1849-1882.
McCabe, Joseph. Journal Unpublished. (San Francisco: Sutro
Branch, State Library).

Newspapers and Periodicals:

Overland Monthly Magazine (San Francisco: Aug. 1904).
Pioneer Monthly Magazine (San Francisco: Jan. to July 1854).
San Francisco Bulletin (San Francisco: Feb. 12, March 1,
1856: Feb. 10, 1858).
San Francisco Daily Herald (San Francisco: June 2, 1852;
April 30, July 17, 27, October 21, 22, 23, 1853).
Wide West Nov. 22, 1857, Feb. 14, 1858, May 18 1856.

CHAPTER VII.

Hauser, Miska. Aus dem Wanderbuche Eines Oesterreichischen
Virtuosen (Leipzig: F. L. Herbig Verlag, 1859).

Newspapers and Periodicals:

Daily Alta California (San Francisco: March 22, Oct. 17, 24,
1852; January 14, 1853; Jan. 31, 1863).
June Music Festival Brochure at De Young Museum, San Francisco, June 1883.
San Francisco Bulletin (San Francisco: Apr. 4, 1856; Sept.
9, 1857; Feb. 19, 1858; May 2, 1859).
San Francisco Daily Herald (San Francisco: July 28, Dec. 24,
1854; May 6, 21, Oct. 26, 1855).
Wide West (San Francisco: Nov. 15, 1857).

CHAPTER VIII.

Mercantile Guide, Business Directory,(San Francisco: 1864).
San Francisco Directory Parker, James M.   (San Francisco:
S. W. Whitton, Towne and Co., 1856).
Newspapers:
San Francisco Call (San Francisco: Oct. 19, 1859).
Wide West (San Francisco: Feb. 18, 1855).

CHAPTER IX.

Howard, John Tasker. Stephen Foster (New York: Thomas Y.
     Crowell, 1934).
Marks, Edward B. They All Sang (New York: Viking Press,
     1935).
Spaeth, Sigmund, and Paskman, Dailey. Gentlemen Be Seated
     (New York: Doubleday-Dorah, 1928).
Spaeth, Sigmund. Read 'Em and Weep (Songs) (New York:Doub-
     leday-Doran, 1935).

Newspapers and Periodicals :

Golden Era, The (San Francisco: Jan.29,
     1854).
Pacific News (San Francisco: Oct.25,27,
     1849).
San Francisco Evening Bulletin (San Francisco: Oct. 25,27,
     1849; May 23, 1856).
San Francisco Bulletin (San Francisco: June and July,1917).

CHAPTER X.

Alverson, Margaret Blake. Sixty Years of California Song
     (San Francisco: Sunset Press, 1913).
Colles, H. C. M.A. (Oxon) Grove's Dictionary of Music and
     Musicians (New York: The MacMillan Co., 1928).
Green, Clay. Memoirs (Mss. of his contributions to various
     newspapers.) Sutro Branch Library, San Francisco.
Hart, Jerome. In Our Second Century (San Francisco:Pioneer
     Press, 1931).
Whelbourne, Hubert. Celebrated Musicians Past and Present
     (New York: Garden City Publishing Co., Inc. 1937).

Newspapers and Periodicals :

Daily Alta California (San Francisco: Jan. 25, 1851;March
     24, 31, July 3, Dec. 1, 1852; April 25, May 15, 1853).
Golden Era, The (San Francisco: Feb. 13, 1853).
Wide West, The (San Francisco: Feb. 11, 1855).
History of Opera in San Francisco (San Francisco: Published
     by San Francisco Theatre Research Project, O.P465-03-286).
San Francisco Bulletin (San Francisco: May 6, 20, 1859).
San Francisco Daily Herald (San Francisco: Sept. 26, 1855).

CHAPTER XI.

Chaplin, Charles. Script of "THE GOLD RUSH" United Artists
     Studio, Hollywood, California.
Dickens, Charles. Household Words (San Francisco: Sept.27,
     1851; March 13, 1859) Vol. 4, p.94.
Dramatic Chronicle (San Francisco: May 25, 1867).

Fetis, Francois Joseph. Biographie Universalle des Musiciens (Paris: Firmin Didot Freres, 1869) 8 Vols. p.316.
Colles, H. C. M. A. (Oxon) Groves Dictionary of Music and Musicians (New York: The MacMillan Co., 1928).
Hauser, Miska. Aus dem Wanderbuche eines oesterreichischen Virtuosen (Leipzig, 1859).
Howard, John F. Our American Music (New York: Thomas Y. Crowell Co., Copyright, 1929, 1929, 30 and 31.)

Newspapers and Periodicals:

Pioneer, The (San Francisco: August 18, 1854).

CHAPTER XII.

Hart, Jerome. In Our Second Century (San Francisco: Pioneer Press, 1931).

Newspapers and Periodicals

Argonaut (San Francisco: Oct. 26, 1878).
Daily Alta California (San Francisco: Feb. 17, 1861.
London News June, 1859.
San Francisco Bulletin (San Francisco: April 5, 1858).
San Francisco Chronicle (San Francisco: Feb. 13, 26, 1856; May 26, 1932).
San Francisco Daily Herald (San Francisco: July 25, 1853).
San Francisco News Letter (San Francisco: Aug. 28, 1875).
Wide West (San Francisco: June 6, 1858).

GENERAL REFERENCE

Langley, Henry G., Comp. City Directories (San Francisco: Commercial Stearn Presses, S. O. Valentine & Son. 1858-63).
Colles, H. C., M. A. (Oxen) Grove's Dictionary of Music and Musicians (New York: The MacMillan Co., 1928).
Thompson, Oscar, Ed., The International Cyclopedia of Music Musicians (New York: Todd, Mead & Co., 1939).
Soule, Frank; Nisbet, James; Gihon, John H. Annals of San Francisco (New York: D. Appleton and Co., 1855).
Bancroft, Robert Howe. History of California (San Francisco: A. L. Bancroft and Co., 1884).

HISTORY OF MUSIC
PROJECT EDITORIAL STAFF
1939

. . . .

MONOGRAPH WRITERS

Harrison Fox   Everett Michael
Ray Graham   Alexandra Pearce

RESEARCH ASSISTANTS
Lula Stickney
Janine Sharman
Donald Cobb
Eric Benson

BIBLIOGRAPHY
Gretchen Clark

PRODUCTION
Margaret Raentsch

PHOTO REPRODUCTION
M. H. McCarty

BLOCK PRINTS
N.Y.A. Art Project under
Franz Brandt's direction

COVER
Courtesy of San Francisco
Federal Music Project

ACKNOWLEDGMENT

Assistance in the technical planning of the
History of Music Project was furnished by
Dr. James B. Sharp, California State Coordi-
nator of Research and Statistical Projects.
Miss Jessica Fredericks, Head of Music Department, San Francisco Public Library, and Miss
Helene Comte, her assistant, have given un-
failing cooperation in matters pertaining
to research, as have Miss Helen Bruner, Sutro
Branch Library, and Miss Mabel Gillis,
Sacramento State Library. Although the entire research and stenographic staff on the
Project assisted in the preparation of this
volume at various stages in production,
particular credit for the writing should be
given to Mr. Harrison Fox, Mr. Ray Graham,
Mr. Everett Michael and Mrs. Alexandra Pearce.

Cornel Lengyel, Editor